Bevan

Clare Beckett is an Associate Professor at the University of Bradford, where she teaches social policy and welfare history. She has particular interest in education for minority and less advantaged students. She is the author of *Thatcher* (Haus 2007).

Francis Beckett is an author, journalist, playwright and contemporary historian. His nineteen books include biographies of four prime ministers: Clement Attlee, Harold Macmillan, Tony Blair and Gordon Brown.

Bevan

by
Clare Beckett
and
Francis Beckett

First published in 2004 by
Haus Publishing
4 Cinnamon Row, London SW11 3TW

This revised paperback edition published in 2024

A CIP catalogue record for this book is available from the British Library

ISBN 978-1-913368-83-8
eISBN 978-1-913368-84-5

Typeset in Garamond by MacGuru Ltd
Printed in the United Kingdom by Clays Ltd, Elcograf S.p.A.

www.hauspublishing.com

Contents

Introduction

F̲ew politicians go to their graves knowing they have done something transformative, but Nye Bevan did. And our book about him is coming out again at just the right time, because Bevan's National Health Service, the achievement for which he will always be remembered, has never been in greater peril than it is now. There is no doubt that another few years of having every fashionable ideology thrown at it as a substitute for investment will be fatal.

Bevan built it on the principle that healthcare should be free at the point of use. The great civilising idea behind it was that no one should be left to die from a treatable illness because they did not have the money to pay for the treatment. He didn't particularly mind the rich having more material goods than the poor. But he had a serious problem with the rich having access to life-saving medical treatment when the poor did not.

At the time, with Hitler just defeated, the right labelled Bevan a Nazi, a would-be Hitler, who aimed to turn Britain's hospitals into concentration camps. That argument has never resurfaced, because it proved to have no traction at all with the public. The NHS is the most popular thing any government has done in our lifetimes. No one has ever again tried to mount a frontal assault on it. It survived the Thatcher years, when – as one of her ministers, Kenneth Baker, put it recently – the government targeted all the reforms of the 1945 Attlee government, and managed over eighteen years to dismantle most of them.

It was clear by then that there were some genuine problems with the Bevan model. It was monolithic, and tried to take on every health monster, from preventative medicine through to cutting edge heart surgery. But Thatcher took an ideological sledgehammer to crack this nut, and the daily work of the NHS has never recovered.

The NHS survived – battered and bruised, but still doing its job. But it was critically weakened. It had been kept short of money, and forced to submit to the prevailing orthodoxy that only markets were worth having by trying to simulate a market. This was called the internal market, and it had everyone in the NHS 'purchasing' services from each other, or from someone else, and competing to 'sell' their services to each other.

Labour came to power in 1997 pledging to get rid of the 'internal market' but fell prey, as Blair's first Health Secretary, the late Frank Dobson, told one of the present authors, to an invalid syllogism: 'Something must be done. This is something. Therefore, this must be done.' Dobson started to dismantle the single market but his work was reversed by his successor, Alan Milburn.

However, Labour in government saved the NHS by giving it priority for money. The jury is out on whether the NHS can withstand the years of Conservative government since 2010. Getting an appointment with a doctor, getting treated in A&E departments, getting lifesaving operations, is harder than it has ever been in the seventy-five-year history of the NHS.

And yet its impact on our national life remains enormous and has been so from the start.

In 1949, the year after it was founded, and the year after the arrival of the HMT Empire Windrush with 600 immigrants aboard, the government began a drive to recruit staff to the NHS from the West Indies.

The NHS inaugurated a polio immunisation programme in 1956 and a whooping cough immunisation programme the following year, and in 1958 a new polio and diphtheria vaccinations programmes ensured that everyone under the age of fifteen was vaccinated. Ten years later it started vaccinating against measles. All these dreadful diseases were pretty well eliminated on these shores. In 1988 it began a programme of free breast screening for all women over fifty, the first of its kind in the world. 1994 saw the establishment of the NHS organ donor programme, and in 2006 came the NHS bowel cancer screening programme for people in their sixties.

Two years later came a vaccine to prevent cervical cancer, available for all girls at the age of twelve, and the huge NHS purchasing power came in handy when the government needed Covid-19 vaccines quickly. The purchase of vaccines, often used by friends of the then Prime Minister Boris Johnson to show that he 'got the big calls right', was much more Nye Bevan's achievement than that of any living politician. Without the NHS it could not have been done.

The NHS transformed the fifties and sixties childhoods of the present authors and those of our generation. It was the greatest achievement of the greatest reforming government Britain has ever known. And it is worth recalling

3

that achievement now, in the 2020s, as we move towards what looks like one of those great watershed moments in British politics that Jim Callaghan talked about. During the 1979 election, Callaghan told an aide, 'There are times, perhaps once every thirty years, when there is a sea-change in politics. It then does not matter what you say or what you do. There is a shift in what the public wants and what it approves of.' He thought he was in the middle of one such moment, and he was right. There were five such moments in the twentieth century, and Keir Starmer could well be swept to power in the first of the twenty-first century.

The twentieth century's five were the Liberal landslide of 1905 and the Conservative one of 1931; Attlee's Labour landslide in 1945, Thatcher's Conservative one in 1979, and Blair's for Labour in 1997. These are moments, not just of a change in government, but of a change in what is politically possible. They have enormous potential.

But the party that benefits from the sea change has to be ready to grasp that potential. That is why Attlee's 1945 government was transformative, and Blair's 1997 government was not. Will Keir Starmer be an Attlee or a Blair? At the time of writing we can't be sure, but we know that he sees the danger the NHS is in. In May 2023, he described what it is like now:

The eight o'clock scramble, the appointments missed, opportunities missed, to spot the pain that turned out to be a tumour. Patients who want to go home, are well enough to go home but who have to stay in hospital for months, waiting for a care package. Day long waits in A&E, record numbers off work sick, people pulling their own teeth out, seven million on waiting, waiting, waiting lists. And ambulances – for heart attack and stroke victims – that don't come in time.[1]

We were, he said, back to the days when the care you got depended on how well off you were: 'In my constituency, a girl born in Highgate Hill will live ten years longer than a girl born in Somers Town. That is three miles away.'[2] To change that, he wants to move care away from hospitals and closer to the community, which means rescuing the GP service.

Bevan's legacy was a network of independent GP practises controlling their own finances, and that worked fine for the Thatcherites too. But Bevan only left it like that because he needed to get the GPs on board – they feared being employed, somehow imagining this reduced their independence. They have learned better now. They know that they don't want to be small business people, they want to spend their time doctoring, and there is a revolution in a small sentence tucked away in Starmer's speech: 'We'll ... make sure salaried GPs serve all communities.' Bevan would be cheering wildly.

If Keir Starmer wants to lead a transformative government, he could do worse than study how Attlee did it, and the appointment of Bevan was key to that. Bevan's political history up to that point was as a left-wing rebel – at one point he was even expelled from the Labour Party. So Attlee's decision to give him a key role in government horrified many people. As we write, Starmer seems to see

Labour's left simply as a problem. Attlee, too, saw it as a problem – but also as a source of energy, drive, and idealism. That's why he was willing to horrify his more orthodox lieutenants by giving Bevan a key job. And having given him a key role, Attlee supported Bevan throughout. Without a Prime Minister who shared his vision, Bevan would have achieved nothing, and would be remembered today, if he was remembered at all, as an interesting left-wing rebel, nothing more.

Clare Beckett
Francis Beckett
May 2023

The Boy from Tredegar

Eight children living with both parents in a small, four-room terraced house did not qualify as poverty in Tredegar, Monmouthshire, when Aneurin (or Nye) Bevan was born there on 15 November 1897. Bevan's family had few material things, but at least his father, David, had work down the mines, the only work available. It provided enough to live on, but it also gave David, as with most miners, the choking black dust disease, pneumoconiosis, that killed him in 1925.

It didn't qualify as poverty, but it was cramped. Bevan's mother, Phoebe, had to use all of her ingenuity and thrift to feed the family properly on what David's long, long days down the mine brought in, as well as supplementing this by working as a seamstress. The Bevans were as well off as anyone around them, and better off than some, but the sense of being a member of an exploited class was with the young Bevan from an early age. When his parents bought their own cottage – something few of their neighbours could do – from the mine owner, Lord Tredegar, the transaction merely proved to the young Bevan how the capitalist class always won: the pit underneath the cottage caused subsidence and they had to spend their evenings propping up the roof. Years later, in 1937, Bevan told the House of Commons that Lord Tredegar, 'having taken out the kernel [i.e. the coal], wanted to sell the shell, that is to say the land.'

David Bevan was a gentle, thoughtful Baptist who loved reading, wrote poetry, sang in the chapel and was treasurer of the local miners' lodge (the union branch). Phoebe, a Methodist, was energetic, practical and strong – she bore ten children (though only six survived to adulthood). She was up before 5 am every day to make her husband's breakfast before he left for the mine (he would not return until after dark); then she would see the children off to school and by 9 am she was ready to start work as a seamstress.

Sirhowy Elementary School, the only school available, boasted the sort of headmaster who was the stuff of nightmares for many working class children of that time. A terrible snob who bullied the children, he valued only rote learning and punished the flights of imagination and unconventional ideas of which the young Bevan was capable. These daily battles probably caused Bevan's severe childhood stutter. It was certainly this philistine pedagogue who advised his parents that the rebellious boy had no chance of passing the eleven-plus examination, which was his only route to secondary school. So in 1911, around his fourteenth birthday, he went down the pit, like his father.

Miners worked desperately hard, for miserable wages, in hideously dangerous conditions. If a collapsing pit didn't get them, then sooner or later the dust did. The misery of being in the dark all day, the physical exhaustion, the fear, were Bevan's constant companions for his nine years down the mine and they stayed with him all his life. If you wanted to see exploitation, greed and human suffering at their most raw, you only had to spend some time in a mining community. Coal was a vital part of the British economy for the first two-thirds of the twentieth century, so miners wielded considerable industrial power and learned how to use it. This is why coal miners became the shock troops of the British Labour movement.

The miners' unions had a mythical status in Labour movement circles for most of the century. They had been starved into defeat in 1926, but took their revenge with a spectacular victory in 1974, which brought down a Conservative government. In 1986, however, they were finally defeated with hideous relish by another Conservative government led by Margaret Thatcher (1925–2013). The century's most inspirational left-wing union leaders all came from the mines: A J Cook (1884–1931) in the 1920s; Arthur Horner (1894– 1969) in the 1930s and 1940s; through to Mick McGahey (1925–1999) and Arthur Scargill (b. 1938) in the 1980s. From the Labour Party's very beginnings, politicians from mining areas crowded onto the Labour benches in Parliament. All of them had been politicized by the awful conditions in the mines.

Now that King Coal has lost his monopoly, we forget how powerful the miners once were. The Conservative minister R A Butler (1902–1982), for instance, used to tell a typical story from the 1950s of a telephone call from Winston Churchill (1874–1965) to say he had settled a dispute with the miners. 'On whose terms, Prime Minister?' asked Butler. 'Ours or theirs?' 'Theirs, of course,' growled Churchill. 'One must have electric light.' And so there is a certain inevitability about the fact that Aneurin Bevan, the politician who was to do so much to shift the balance of power in favour of the underdog, became politicized after following his father down a South Wales mine.

Bevan was always the one who argued most with the overmen who supervised the work in the colliery. In the evenings he read voraciously, borrowing books from the Workmen's Institute, or he argued for more militant policies at meetings of the local lodge of the South Wales Miners' Federation. In 1916, aged only nineteen, he became the youngest ever chairman of the lodge.

The First World War had begun in 1914, but Bevan was convinced that the war was not a straightforward struggle between good and evil, as the Government wanted people to believe. He saw earlier than many of his contemporaries that the causes of the War were far more complex than the evil lunacy of the Kaiser and he proved impervious to the jingoistic propaganda provided by the Government.

Bevan managed to avoid being called up to fight on the grounds of ill health: he had the miners' eye disease nystagmus, which results in rapid, involuntary movements of the eye. As a result he never had to make the stark decision that confronted so many of his generation: whether to fight in the war or risk prison for refusing to fight. In 1914 Clement Attlee, the man who was to lead the 1945 Labour government, chose to go to the front; on the other hand, the man who became Attlee's deputy, Herbert Morrison, chose the odium of being a conscientious objector or 'conchie', as they were called.

Bevan continued to work down the mine. So, unlike many of his generation – including his future colleagues Attlee and Morrison – he was not scarred by the experience of serving on the Western Front or persecuted as a 'conchie'. Instead, by the time the war ended in 1918, Bevan was a well-known figure in the South Wales Miners' Federation. This brash young man made enemies quickly, but friends even more quickly, and he rose rapidly in the union. More importantly, the twenty-two-year-old Bevan had won a scholarship (offered by the Federation) to the Central Labour College in London, where promising young trade unionists could learn about Labour Party history and Marxist economics. Though he could not know it at the time, Bevan would never go down a mine again.

To Bevan, it was like winning the lottery. Yet, as it turned out, his two years at the Labour College proved disappointing. The principal, W W Craik, found Bevan the most problematic of all his students that year and thought this might be a hangover from Bevan's dislike of school. Bevan skipped lectures and preferred taking long walks through the streets of London, that huge, strange, cold city, as well as debating the political issues of the time late into the night with his fellow students.

Slowly, with the help of the college's visiting elocution tutor, Bevan conquered his stutter, which would surely have snuffed out his political career before it had even begun. For the first time in his life, he had time to study, to think and to read without being exhausted from a hard day's work down the mine. The scholarship gave him a chance to refine his political ideas and to broaden his reading beyond what was available at the Tredegar Workmen's Institute. For instance, he decided that Marx's *Communist Manifesto* was for all rebels an inspiration and a weapon, but today tactically valueless, except insofar as persistent stress on first principles is of tactical importance.'[3]

It also helped him to think through the answer to the question which, he wrote later, preyed on his mind more than any other:

Where was power and which was the road to it? It wasn't an individual question – 'How do I lay my hands on power?' – but a question posed on behalf of the working class, for society presented itself to us as an arena of conflicting social forces and not as a plexus of individual striving.[4]

Back in Tredegar, the twenty-three-year-old Bevan had to give his first thoughts to his family. His father had developed the choking cough that would soon kill him and was often too ill to work. On the other hand, Bevan could get no work, for the company that owned the mine said it had nothing for him. A wave of militancy in mining areas had only recently been quelled and it is likely that the Tredegar Iron and Coal Company had Bevan down as a troublemaker.

The mines had been nationalized during the war as an emergency measure, but now the Government went back on its promise to implement the recommendation of a Royal Commission to keep them that way. In 1919, an army of men were returning from the trenches and the terrible weapon of unemployment was thrust into the mineowners' hands. They did not hesitate to use it against any man who preached industrial unrest. 'From its wartime zenith of prosperity and confidence, South Wales plunged in a few years to a nadir of poverty and despair,' says John Campbell, one of Bevan's more recent, and least sympathetic, biographer.[5] Wages declined, membership of the South Wales Miners' Federation halved and the pits closed.

With the exception of a couple of short breaks, Bevan was out of work for three years. At first he received ten shillings a week unemployment pay from the state, but when his sister, Arianwen, returned from college and got a job as a stenographer on £2 a week, the rules stated that Bevan had to live on her income and forego his ten shillings. His father was now so ill that he could not even work as an insurance agent, which had brought in a little money now that he was too ill to mine, and his sickness benefit was also refused because of Arianwen's job. But this decision was reversed after the young Bevan complained to the authorities. In fact, he argued his case with such skill that his mother began scheming to find a way for her son to read for the Bar. For the remaining two years of David Bevan's life, he at least had the dignity of a tiny income until one terrible day in February 1925 he choked to death in his son's arms.

It was a wretched time. Bevan became an expert in the workings of the mean and demeaning social security system, helping his father and many others to get the best they could from it. And he became a leading light in Tredegar's emerging Labour Party. He read more and more socialist theory and, with a group of friends his own age, he planned to take over the local council, then the world.

His first political office came at the age of twenty-five. Councillor Bevan of Tredegar Urban District Council – occupation: 'unemployed miner' (as it said on the ballot paper) – was soon working and campaigning for better housing and lower rents and attacking the only important employer in the town, the Tredegar Iron and Coal Company. When Councillor Bevan and his friends took control of the Workmen's Institute, he became chairman of the committee that ran the library that had done so much to furnish his adolescent mind. They organized demonstrations against the low levels of unemployment pay and the humiliations heaped upon the growing army of men who had been forced to ask for it.

In time, however, Tredegar became too small for Bevan and his friends and they extended their activities to the whole parliamentary constituency of which it was a part – Ebbw Vale, a federation of the three villages in three neighbouring valleys: Tredegar, Rhymney and the biggest, Ebbw Vale village itself. Bevan became the chairman of the Constituency Labour Party in 1923. A few months later, Ramsay MacDonald became Prime Minister at the head of the first-ever Labour government.

In 1926 Bevan began to earn a small income from his union and political work. He was appointed disputes agent and the lodge members contributed a penny a week to give him a wage of £5 a week. It was more than most miners earned, but the lodge members got their money's worth: his sister Arianwen acted as Bevan's secretary, while his mother moved to a bigger house so as to give him an office, with a telephone.

Bevan's new career had hardly begun when he was plunged into the worst explosion of class conflict Britain had ever experienced: the General Strike. In April 1926 mine owners demanded longer hours for less pay. A row had been brewing for months and the national miners' leader Arthur Cook had tramped the country with his inspirational message: 'Not a penny off the pay, not a minute on the day.' On 2 May 1926 the Conservative Prime Minister, Stanley Baldwin (1867–1947), broke off negotiations with the Trades Union Congress (TUC) delegation. The TUC called out its members in support of the miners, who refused to accept a pay cut, and for nine days (3–12 May 1926) the nation ground to a halt.

As the strike took hold, Bevan was optimistic that the mine owners might be defeated, but the Government was well-prepared for a General Strike and managed to keep essential services going. The TUC leaders surrendered unconditionally. It was a bitter blow for the unions; especially the miners, who were left to fight on alone.

That is what they did in South Wales where Bevan organized the Relief Committee, which tried to ensure his members were not starved back to work. Arthur Cook saw the way the wind was blowing and was prepared to accept a face-saving formula if he could get one – to the fury of men like Bevan, who wanted to hold out for a better deal. 'We say there are possibilities and probabilities of more favourable terms in the near future,' Bevan had insisted on his first appearance at a national miners' conference. But there was nothing of the kind, as Cook saw more clearly than the angry man of twenty-nine who attacked him.

Not that it made any practical difference. There was no face-saving formula. The mine owners sensed total victory and were not inclined to be magnanimous about it.

Bevan was now a national figure in the mining union. He visited a Nottinghamshire coalfield to try to prevent the drift back to work that had begun there, but the threat of starvation had its effect much wider than Nottinghamshire. A few weeks after he had talked of possibilities and probabilities, he was forced to admit they did not exist. Once he realized this, he acted upon it with something that marked him out from many of the angry young men in the union: a good politician's instinct for the possible. The next time a national conference was called, he told delegates it was time to bow to the inevitable. They did.

Bevan's life was now at a crossroads, though he may not have seen it clearly at the time. The next logical step for a union activist of his standing was to become a full-time official in the union and he might have done just that. But history, especially political history, is full of 'ifs'. If a union official's post had become vacant, Bevan might well have applied for it successfully and would probably have risen to become the union's national leader. History would then remember Nye Bevan as a mining union leader in 1945 who helped shape the nationalization of the mines, rather than as the minister who created the National Health Service; and both these events might well have assumed a very different form.

Instead, a growing dissatisfaction among the miners with the sitting Labour MP for Ebbw Vale gave Bevan's friends the chance to put his name forward for Parliament. He was selected as the Labour candidate and on 1 June 1929 the thirty-one-year-old Nye Bevan was elected to Parliament by a huge majority.

Bevan the parliamentarian was born. After the brutal defeat of the General Strike it seemed like the only route open to him. As he wrote many years later, the strike had ended a phase in his life and from then on the pendulum had swung towards political action: 'It seemed to us that we must try to regain in parliament what we had lost on the industrial battlefield.'[6]

The Making of a Parliamentarian

'There are about fifty miners' members in the new Parliament, but I do not think Aneurin Bevan will be exactly lost in the crowd,' wrote the *Daily Herald*'s political correspondent in June 1929. Bevan's biographer John Campbell writes of the difference between the angry young man from Tredegar and other mining MPs. They were typically quiet, gentle souls, he says, like Bevan's future cabinet colleague Jim Griffiths (1890–1975), 'the soul of gentleness, moderation and conciliation, a chapel-going, Welsh-speaking Welshman whose socialism was ethical and compassionate, not angry and theoretical.'[7]

But it was Bevan, not Griffiths, who represented the spirit of the pitheads in 1929. If more mining MPs were not like Bevan it was because men like Bevan were normally considered too valuable for Parliament and were needed to organize the mining trade union. Promising young firebrands went to work in union offices, where they believed the real business of the working class was done. Trade unions from the 1920s to the 1970s, and to some extent even today, regarded Labour MPs as rather wayward junior partners who had their occasional uses – a bit like journalists. Often the big unions looked upon a parliamentary seat as a reasonable consolation prize for someone who was no longer up to the arduous work of trade union organization. Bevan had followed his own instinct that power was to be found in Westminster. His union colleagues believed power was to be found in the traditional weapon of the working class: trade union organization.

Anyway, Bevan was not numbered among the angriest of the firebrands in the dispiriting parliament of 1929–1931. The first choice he had to make was whether to align himself with the rebels in the Independent Labour Party (ILP), once the heart of the parliamentary Labour Party but increasingly now a left-wing opposition to the leadership. At the very beginning of the 1929 parliament, the ILP took a decision that immediately put it at odds with Ramsay MacDonald's Labour government. It insisted its MPs should vote in accordance with ILP policies, even when they conflicted with those of the Labour Party (as everybody knew they would).

The result was that only eighteen of its 140 MPs stayed with the ILP, which from then on was effectively a separate party. Bevan could have thrown in his lot with the rebels right from the start. He chose not to though, as a socialist whose whole reason for entering parliament was to change fundamentally the balance of wealth and power in Britain, he knew MacDonald's government was going to be a disappointment.

Though it had no overall parliamentary majority, the Government had real power – if it chose to use it. Theoretically, the Conservatives and Liberals with 320 MPs could combine and vote down the Labour government (which had 287 MPs), thereby precipitating another general election. MacDonald was quick to remind Labour MPs of this whenever they asked for more radical policies.

No senior Liberal wanted to precipitate an early election. The longer it could be deferred, the greater the chance their party's fortunes might revive. In any case the Liberals had produced a programme to deal with unemployment which involved public works on a huge scale, so they could hardly have opposed radical measures on unemployment, had MacDonald been minded to introduce any.

The Conservatives were not looking for an early election, either. Conservative leader Stanley Baldwin faced serious internal dissent fomented by the owners of Britain's major newspapers. He also calculated that the dire economic circumstances, as well as MacDonald's own inclinations, would render the Labour government harmless.

So, despite its lack of an overall majority, the Labour government could have introduced radical measures, but MacDonald – Prime Minister for the second time at the age of sixty-two – made his intentions clear with his choice of ministers. 'The general impression left by a study of its personnel,' noted *The Times* newspaper, 'is that it is the best that could have been designed to carry out the unprovocative policy which is apparently to mark the beginning of the new Labour regime, and which the circumstances of the moment certainly render desirable.' Arthur Henderson (1863–1935), who had created Labour's electoral machine, was Foreign Secretary; Philip Snowden (1864–1937) was a very conservative Chancellor of the Exchequer; and railwaymen's union leader Jimmy Thomas (1874–1949) was Lord Privy Seal with the task of finding a cure for unemployment.

The most notable absentee from the list of MacDonald's ministers was the one member of his first government who had actually made a difference: his health and housing minister, the left-wing ILP leader John Wheatley (1869–1930). Wheatley's Housing Act had for the first time started to address the problems of slums. In a pre-election list of possible ministerial appointments, Wheatley was pencilled in for the Ministry of Labour, but by the time the election results were declared MacDonald had decided he could afford to keep Wheatley out. *The Daily Express* saw this omission, rightly, as a declaration of war on the Left.

Wheatley, now sixty, was a name to conjure within socialist circles. He was the political hero of Bevan's father, who on his deathbed had asked for a copy of the *Daily Herald* so he could read out about Wheatley's latest doings. Bevan, too, had admired Wheatley from afar and was inclined to support his early criticisms of the Government. At the first meeting of the new parliamentary Labour Party, Wheatley had prophesied an economic crisis, with the Labour government scrabbling to take money from the poorest whom they had been elected to defend: which is exactly what happened.

Wheatley's life has some remarkable parallels with Bevan's own, from his birth to his ministerial career. In fact, Bevan could be seen as the man who continued the work that Wheatley began. Like Bevan, Wheatley followed his father down the mines – in Scotland rather than Wales – and worked there for fifteen years. A grim, poverty-stricken childhood and friendships with socialists like James Connolly (1868–1916) – a frequent visitor to the Wheatley household, until his execution by the British for being one of the main leaders of the Easter Rising in Dublin

(1916) – combined to add the socialist faith to his Catholic one. The two faiths coexisted uneasily: the Catholic Church in Scotland regarded socialism as godless and wicked, while Scottish socialists saw Catholics as reactionaries whose only aim was to keep the workers in their place by telling them to wait patiently for a better life in the next world.

In 1901, the thirty-two-year-old Wheatley became a reporter and then an advertising canvasser for a Catholic newspaper, the *Glasgow observer*. Five years later he started a printing business. It prospered and made him fairly rich, allowing him in 1923 to found a weekly newspaper, the *Glasgow Evening Standard*, which lasted until 1960.

Well before the First World War, Wheatley and James Maxton (1885–1946) had become (as they were to remain until 1930) the joint leaders of the ILP and were both elected to Parliament in the 1922 general election.

Wheatley's strength in the House of Commons was his close reasoning and mastery of detail. He was not a flamboyant orator like Maxton, but he could hold the House in his spell in a way Maxton never could. In the short-lived 1924 Labour government, Wheatley took the job that was later to give Bevan his place in history: Minister of Health and Housing. Wheatley's Housing Act, which provided for a steadily expanding investment in public housing at modest rents, was that government's chief – if not its only – achievement.

After the 1924 Labour government fell, it was Wheatley who ensured that in future the ILP would be the vehicle for left-wing opposition to MacDonald, just as Bevan was to play a key role in the Socialist League after 1931.

Wheatley was short, dumpy and unprepossessing, peering myopically through thick, round spectacles. Maxton was his opposite: painfully thin, handsome and romantic in a raddled sort of way, with long, flowing black hair; an eloquent former schoolteacher whose spellbinding oratory was legendary and who lived on his nerves and a constant supply of tea and cigarettes.

Maxton, at the start of the parliament, put forward the demands of the Left: 'I am going to promise the Cabinet active hearty support and work on one condition and one condition only, that they will arrange the affairs of this country that no unemployed man, his wife or child, shall have any dread of starvation or insult.'

Unemployment rose from 1,630,000 in June 1929 to 1,912,000 in June 1930. Well before the end of the year it had topped the two million mark and was still rising (it reached three million by the time the second Labour government fell). By midsummer Maxton was asking the House of Commons: 'Has any human being benefited by the fact that there has been a Labour Government in office?' In October he said: 'It would be foolish to expect the Government to deliver socialism but ... the Government had it in their power to stop starvation.'

If Bevan had been simply the angry, dogmatic firebrand depicted by the biographer John Campbell, he would instantly have thrown in his lot with the eighteen ILP MPs. In fact, the ILP's attempts to recruit him failed, though he often voted with them. ILP members dismissed Bevan as 'an armchair revolutionary', partly because he hated getting up early in the morning. He had also acquired some expensive tastes for things he had never had before: now he could afford occasional meals at the Café Royal.

He carefully cultivated a rather surprising set of parliamentary friends, only one of whom was identified with the Left – and he was a wealthy old Etonian, John Strachey (1901–1963). Other friends included the lively young Liberal MP Frank Owen, whom Bevan had known in Wales when Owen was a reporter on the *South Wales Weekly Argus* and with whom Bevan shared a London flat above a garage in Cromwell Road, Kensington. He also befriended a young Conservative, Edward Marjoribanks, the stepson of the first Lord Hailsham, who introduced him to Lord Beaverbrook, proprietor of the *Daily Express, Sunday Express* and *Evening Standard*.

Bevan's friendship with Beaverbrook led to raised eyebrows in Labour circles, for Beaverbrook was fiercely right wing and utterly cynical and manipulative. He cultivated a few young, left-wing politicians, but the future Prime Minister Clement Attlee thought Beaverbrook corrupted them with his lavish hospitality. Bevan did not think it was corruption. As Michael Foot puts it: 'Bevan could enjoy all the good things rich hosts could provide.'[8] But the taunt by the journalist and Conservative politician Brendan Bracken (1901–1958) – appropriately over Beaverbrook's dinner table – has stuck to Bevan:

'You Bollinger Bolshevik, you ritzy Robespierre, you lounge-lizard Lenin, look at you, swilling Max's champagne and calling yourself a socialist.'[9]

It was unquestionably a dangerous relationship. Attlee was right about that. Beaverbrook liked people to be in his debt and Bevan was forced in the 1930s first to decline Beaverbrook's offer of private medical assistance when he was ill and then to refuse an offer of a cottage on his estate. Bevan's letter to Beaverbrook regarding the latter suggests that his refusal was reluctant.

Bevan made a cautious first contribution in the House. He asked the Prime Minister to do something about the 'iniquities' of the unemployment insurance system, a subject he knew a great deal about, having had to fight the system to obtain unemployment benefit for himself and many of his friends as well as sick pay for his father. His second contribution was to defend, of all people, the union leader Jimmy Thomas (whom the ILP considered beyond redemption) against attacks from Conservatives and Liberals. Bevan badgered the Government on small points and supported it on the big issues.

But it could not last. If you wanted to change the world, supporting MacDonald's government was no way to achieve it. On all the matters Bevan cared about, the Government was doing nothing. Jimmy Thomas, who had been given the task of halting the great tidal wave of unemployment, was disintegrating before his colleagues' eyes. A man who owed his political career to his superficial joviality, he was petrified by the enormity of the task and was drinking too much and offering nothing but trite pieces of homespun wisdom.

The Government could not halt unemployment. And since the Chancellor of the Exchequer Philip Snowden was committed to orthodox finance, it could not make the lives of the unemployed any easier. In fact, to the horror of the ILP, the Government set out to make things even harder.

When Lord Rothermere's newspapers printed horror stories of people getting a few shillings from the dole to which they were not entitled, the impressionable MacDonald began talking of married women turning up to collect their dole money wearing fur coats. As a consequence it was made even harder to claim unemployment benefit.

Rebellion looked increasingly attractive. As ILP members became even more unpopular with orthodox Labour members, Bevan found himself voting with them more frequently. But everything changed when, on 12 May 1930, John Wheatley unexpectedly died. Maxton took over sole leadership of the ILP, but, as Michael Foot writes, 'Wheatley's death was a near-mortal blow to the Left. Maxton without Wheatley was a different and lesser man.'[10]

Bevan might well have grown closer to the ILP had Wheatley lived, but he could not bring himself to follow Maxton. For a while he teetered on the edge of making a dreadful mistake. It must have seemed to him that the mantle of John Wheatley had fallen on one of Wheatley's admirers, an immensely rich, clever, charming young aristocrat who had resigned from Jimmy Thomas's unemployment team in despair and put forward his own scheme for dealing with the problem, which involved a huge programme of public works. That man was Sir Oswald Mosley.

Mosley took his scheme to the parliamentary Labour Party and to the annual conference. They turned him down and he published the *Mosley Memorandum*, which was signed by seventeen Labour MPs, including Bevan.

Mosley's followers – prominent among them Bevan (who had evidently decided Mosley was a more credible leader of the Left than Maxton) – issued another appeal to the Labour Party to support Mosley's proposals. His supporters now numbered just five: Bevan, John Strachey, Oliver Baldwin (the left-wing son of the Conservative leader Stanley Baldwin), Robert Forgan, and W J Brown.

But Mosley's thoughts had turned towards creating a new political party, the so-called New Party. Baldwin, Forgan and Strachey went with him and the four of them resigned from the Labour Party. W J Brown almost went and dropped out of the Labour Party, effectively ending his political career. That left Bevan.

He was suddenly desperately isolated. He was not one of the ILP, though he frequently voted with them. He was not a MacDonald loyalist either. Mosley had seemed to offer what Bevan had hoped for from John Wheatley and Maxton: a realistic and effective alternative to MacDonald. Bevan and his closest parliamentary friend, John Strachey, had supported Mosley thus far. He had helped write the manifesto on which the New Party was based. Would he go the extra mile and follow Strachey out of the Labour Party?

Strachey was more than a friend. He was a mentor and guide, a man whose life could not have been more different from Bevan's, yet who had reached the same conclusions and had all the knowledge and sophistication that went with privilege. Their relationship can be gauged by an extraordinary and uncharacteristic letter Bevan wrote to Strachey in October 1930:

It hurts me a little that you give so much and I can give nothing in return. So few people have given me

28

anything that I feel a little strange and bewildered.
I count our friendship as the one thing of value that
membership of parliament has given me ... I am so
conscious of bringing to our relationship nothing of
value, and, therefore, am frightened of trusting so
much of my affection in so ill-balanced a vessel.[11]

If Strachey – who had worked closely with Mosley since
1925 – judged the time was right to take a huge step into
the political unknown with him, could Strachey's friend
and disciple Bevan refuse to go too?

He could and he did. Bevan was the very last of Mosley's supporters to pull out and he did so just in time.
In fact, staying as long as he did proved almost fatal to
his political career. The MP Jennie Lee claims that Bevan
predicted Mosley's destination would be a British variant
of Fascism and perhaps he did; but the real reason for
his refusal to join the New Party is summed up neatly
by John Campbell: 'It was the one absolute and unshake-
able fundamental of Bevan's philosophy ... that there was
no hope of socialism or salvation for the British working
class except through the Labour Party and the organized
labour movement.'[12]

In the first few months of 1931 the state of the British
economy worsened almost by the minute. British banks
had taken short-term loans from the Americans and the
French and lent to the Germans at higher rates of interest. When the German banks failed, the British were left
deeply in debt to the French and the Americans. By February Philip Snowden was telling the House of Commons:

'The national position is so grave that drastic and disagreeable measures will have to be taken.' Labour MPs knew he meant a reduction in unemployment benefits.

The following month the Prime Minister set up a committee chaired by Sir George May (1871–1946), secretary of the Prudential Insurance Company, to recommend 'all possible reductions in national expenditure'. There was only one place all this could end.

The May Committee report was published on 1 August 1931. Sir George May said that the only possible solution was to save £97 million of national expenditure by cutting unemployment benefit and teachers' and police salaries by 20 per cent. MacDonald and Snowden released the report without comment or policy statement. Throughout August the drift from sterling accelerated and the political bandwagon for cutting unemployment benefit, propelled by the right-wing newspapers, the banks and the Conservatives, rapidly became unstoppable.

The Left and the trade unions wanted to know whether the entire £97 million had to come from the unemployed, from social services and from the pay of public servants such as teachers and policemen. Several Cabinet members and the TUC wanted at least some of it to come from those who lived on investments or on property. They thought the rich ought to pay as well as the poor – including the city financiers, whose greedy strategy had collapsed and who had then run to the Government to demand that the unemployed and public servants should pay the price.

MacDonald struggled for a compromise. On the morning of Thursday 20 August 1931 he presented a package to

Conservative and Liberal leaders, who rejected it as insufficiently draconian. That afternoon he put it to the TUC general council, who rejected it as too draconian.

The Prime Minister and his closest colleagues were furious – not with the Conservative and Liberal leaders, but with the TUC. 'The General Council are pigs,' said the socialist economist Sidney Webb (1859–1947) to his wife Beatrice (1858–1943). 'They won't agree to any cuts of unemployment insurance benefits or salaries or wages.'[13] But how – Bevan might have asked – could he have expected them to? The Government was proposing the very measures that the TUC had founded the Labour Party to oppose. And the General Council believed – rightly, most people now acknowledge – that Snowden's measures would not have been successful. The TUC's alternative was the suspension of the sinking fund for the national debt and new taxes on investments. TUC opposition ensured the resistance of the trade unionists in the Cabinet, in particular that of the foreign secretary Arthur Henderson.

By the end of August 1931 MacDonald and Snowden were sure that Britain's salvation depended entirely on obtaining a loan from a New York bank. The bank told Snowden there must be a 10 per cent cut in unemployment benefit or there would be no loan. The Cabinet turned this down by twelve votes to nine. MacDonald, 'looking scared and unbalanced', according to Harold Nicolson in his biography of George V, went to the palace to advise the King to summon the other party leaders. But Baldwin and acting Liberal leader Sir Herbert Samuel (1870–1963) believed the best solution was a new 'National Government' consisting of all three parties and led by MacDonald. If unpopular measures hurting Labour's natural constituency were to be introduced, it would be convenient to have Labour implicated. MacDonald put up a token resistance to the flattering idea that he was the indispensable man and then on Monday morning, 24 August 1931, he told the Cabinet that he 'could not refuse the King's request' to lead the National Government.

MacDonald, Snowden and Thomas entered a coalition government with the Conservatives. They were immediately expelled from the Labour Party and the sixty-eight-year-old Arthur Henderson was elected unopposed as Labour leader. Lingering hopes that MacDonald might not call a snap election, which could destroy the party to which he owed his career, were swiftly dashed. The Government secured the American loan, abandoned the gold standard which it had been formed to safeguard and made the reductions in unemployment benefit and public service pay which MacDonald's Labour colleagues had refused to make. Then, six weeks after he had formed his National Government, MacDonald dissolved Parliament for an election.

The public had had a bad scare and with some justice put it down to the incompetence of the Labour government. The fact that the two chief figures in that government were Prime Minister and Chancellor of the Exchequer in the National Government mattered little, because now they stood alongside the reassuring figures of the Conservative Stanley Baldwin and the Liberal Herbert Samuel.

The National Government was returned with 556 seats and a majority of 500 over all opposition parties. Labour won a mere forty-six seats. It was the most crushing defeat imaginable for a party which, just two years before, had been the biggest party in the House of Commons.

Labour's leadership was decimated. Arthur Henderson lost his seat, along with a huge swathe of his colleagues. Veteran left-winger George Lansbury (1859–1940) became Labour leader at the age of seventy-two and the only other survivor with any ministerial experience, Clement Attlee – who had become Postmaster General just five months before the Labour government collapsed – became deputy leader.

The Labour vote in South Wales held up better than in the rest of the country and Bevan was returned unopposed in Ebbw Vale. But the Left, of which Bevan was now identifiably a part, was in a parlous condition. The eighteen ILP members had found official Labour candidates put up against them in their constituencies, which normally resulted in a Conservative victory, and Maxton and just two others were back in Parliament.

Bevan surveyed the wreckage of the Left. Strachey had broken from Mosley and was heading fast towards Communism, where many of Labour's left-wingers were going. Mosley, too, was proving popular with many disillusioned Labour people. Maxton led the ILP out of the Labour Party and it dwindled as it fought a bitter, vitriolic and ultimately a losing battle against the Communist Party.

Among Maxton's ILP colleagues was Bevan's new best friend. Jennie Lee, the daughter of a Scottish miner, was to have a far greater effect on his life and thinking than even Strachey had done. Jennie had become MP for North

Lanark at the age of twenty-four and lost her seat in 1931 when she had to fight not only the Conservatives but also (because she remained loyal to Maxton and the ILP) the official Labour Party. She was an ex-MP at only twenty-six, nine years younger than Bevan.

Jennie had taken a different path from Bevan and it had cost her her seat. They argued fiercely about it. 'And you, where do you think you're heading?' Bevan asked her as he strode restlessly about her London flat:

> Why don't you get yourself to a nunnery and be done with it? My poor Salvation Army lassie ... I tell you it's the Labour Party or nothing ... I know all its faults and all its dangers ... and I am by no means convinced that something cannot yet be made of it.[14]

Bevan and Jennie had known each other well during the 1929–1931 Parliament, but his closest political and personal friendships were with men like Strachey and Frank Owen. Jennie was friendly with Maxton and the ILP group and her closest personal relationship was with the ILP member Frank Wise (1885–1933), with whom she was having an intense affair. After 1931, with Jennie out of Parliament and more aware of Maxton's weaknesses as well as his strengths, and Bevan increasingly a standard-bearer of the new parliamentary Left, she and Bevan grew closer with each passing week, but only as friends and colleagues.

Then, in November 1933, Frank Wise suddenly collapsed and died of a brain haemorrhage. Jennie was devastated. Bevan was one of a small group of people who tried to look after her and she wrote to a friend: 'Aneurin and [drama critic Hubert] Griffiths are both good pals. They take me anywhere I want to go, but they are not Frank.' Bevan, she wrote, 'is as unreliable as Frank was reliable. He is moody, self-indulgent, but in a curious way he is a brother to me. Our mining background, outlooks, hopes and despairs are most similar.'[15]

Bevan worked hard to change that relationship. Years later, Jennie withdrew her comments about Bevan, saying how little she knew him when she wrote them, but Frank Wise was the true love of her life.

In October 1934, Jennie and Bevan married at Holborn Registry Office; quietly, with Bevan's old friend and supporter from Tredegar, Archie Rush, as best man. Bevan was thirty-six and Jennie was twenty-nine. It was a durable and remarkable personal and political partnership that lasted for the rest of Bevan's life. They pooled their resources and bought a ramshackle Tudor cottage on Brimpton Common, Berkshire, which they restored mostly with their own hands.

There were many who argued that all 1931 showed was the treachery of MacDonald. Others, like Bevan, thought it showed that parliamentary democracy could never deliver a fairer society. This view pushed many socialists towards Communism and sometimes Fascism. Even Attlee started to argue that the next Labour government would have to take emergency powers the moment it was elected, to control the flight of capital.

After 1932, what remained of the Labour Party Left congregated in the newly formed Socialist League. Its leading light was the patrician figure of Sir Richard Stafford Cripps (1889–1952), the only former minister left on the Labour benches in the House of Commons apart from the leader and deputy leader, Lansbury and Attlee. Cripps subsidized the League from his enormous wealth – he had inherited a fortune, married another and earned a third as one of the leading barristers of his day. He was also the League's intellectual powerhouse; and he inherited its leadership by virtue of his connections, for he was related to Sidney and Beatrice Webb, which made him something like royalty in Labour Party circles.

The Socialist League was Bevan's obvious political home, yet he hesitated about joining. He never was a natural rebel, a Maxton or a Tony Benn (1925–2014). Jennie was, but not Bevan. The Labour Party – the official party of drab, cautious trade unionists – was in his bones. Leaving it was inconceivable and even rebelling against its leadership was never what he wanted to do with his political life. In his view the Labour Party remained the one hope for the class he was in Parliament to represent. He was a practical politician and had come to Parliament seeking the power to change how the world was run.

But Bevan joined the Socialist League in the end. He could see little alternative and at least it was determined to work within the established Labour Party, unlike the ILP. He even grew to like and admire Cripps. And the mass unemployment of the early 1930s, which hit South Wales especially hard, seemed to Bevan to demand a response from the party of the working class that went beyond the cautious parliamentary gradualism which was starting to reassert itself in the party of Lansbury and Attlee. To fail to provide it would have been to hand the field over to those of his former parliamentary colleagues who had seen no hope except on the fringes of politics – and were now to be found among the Communists and the Fascists.

As a social worker in London's East End, Clement Attlee had witnessed the desperate poverty of the working class. It had made him a socialist, but that was not quite the same as seeing it among one's friends and neighbours, as Bevan had. In 1933, when the Government introduced an Insurance Bill designed to bring order to the unemployment benefits system, Bevan attacked it with the passion of a man who knew every misery and humiliation it would bring to his friends, neighbours and relatives. The principle in the Bill that a man must look to his family for support 'eats like an acid into the homes of the poor,' he said. 'In the small rooms and around the meagre tables of the poor, hells of personal acrimony and wounded vanities arise' – and he knew what he was talking about.

So, almost despite himself, Bevan was on the side of the rebels. He could never join the Communist Party, but he could not refuse to support a march or demonstration in support of the unemployed simply because it was organized by Communists, as was often the case.

This brought him nothing but abuse from both sides. The Communists, obsessed with rigid ideological purity and inclined to attack the Left of the Party more fiercely than the Right, accused Bevan of having sold out to capitalism. Labour loyalists, on the other hand, sneered that he ought to join the Communists. 'Much of the confusion that exists in the minds of the rank and file,' the back-bench MP Emmanuel Shinwell (1884–1984) told Labour's 1934 conference, 'is due to the innuendoes and insinuations of men like Aneurin Bevan. If Bevan or anyone else believes that the Party is insipid or lacking in courage ... then in my judgement they ought to join the Party or organization which they believe has got the attributes that the Labour Party ought to have.' Herbert Morrison at the same conference mocked 'individuals in the Party who think they are greater than the Party as a whole'. The conference agreed a resolution, aimed partly at Bevan, which sought to prevent Labour MPs from appearing on platforms organized by Communists. Bevan ignored it.

Unemployment and its consequences were the central features of Bevan's life and work from 1931 to 1934. But by 1934, even unemployment was beginning to be over-shadowed by events abroad. Adolf Hitler (1883–1945) was appointed German Chancellor in January 1933 and at the Labour conference the following year the Socialist League took a position of absolute pacifism and unilateral disarmament.

Labour leader George Lansbury (1859–1940) was a life-long pacifist, but he was soon facing demands that the Party should support rearmament. They came from no less a figure than Ernest Bevin, the leader of Britain's biggest trade union, the Transport and General Workers' Union – and the man whom people always confuse with Aneurin Bevan.

In September 1935 the TUC, under Ernest Bevin's tute-lage, resolved that if the Italian Fascist dictator Benito Mussolini (1883–1945) invaded Abyssinia he must be stopped

– by force if necessary. This was also the attitude of the Government. On 3 October 1935 Italy invaded Abyssinia. Two days later Labour's annual conference, which was meeting at the time in Brighton, debated a resolution calling for sanctions against Italy and for League of Nations intervention. Lansbury opposed it.

Attacking the elderly, decent and idealistic Lansbury at that moment was going to look like abusing St Theresa and only one man in Britain could have contemplated it: Ernest Bevin, the most powerful trade union leader in British history, waddled to the platform. 'I hope this conference will not be influenced by either sentiment or personal attachment,' he said. 'It is placing the Executive and the Labour movement in an absolutely wrong position to be taking your conscience round from body to body asking to be told what to do with it.' The motion was carried and Lansbury resigned as leader on 8 October 1935.

Bevan had stood with Lansbury, Cripps and the Socialist League, not with Bevin. Unlike Lansbury, however, Bevan was not a pacifist. Michael Foot (who is reluctant to accept that his hero ever made a mistake) tries to explain Bevan's attitude by saying that, with remarkable prescience, he saw that the Government, whatever it said, had no real intention of doing anything to protect Abyssinia – which turned out to be the case. But this is rationalization with hindsight and even Foot is forced to admit that the 'core of the case put by Cripps and Bevan was the fear that the Labour movement would be sucked into a full bi-partisan defence and foreign policy with a capitalist government whose purposes they could neither share nor control.'[16] It was an understandable view from the British Left, scarred by its memories of the First World War (still, in those days, 'the Great War'). But the truth is not that Bevan brilliantly foretold that the Government would let down Abyssinia, but that he was willing to do so himself.

On 19 October 1935, eleven days after Lansbury's resignation, taking full advantage of Labour's disarray, Prime Minister Stanley Baldwin announced that the general election would be held on 14 November 1935. Labour was leaderless and publicly divided, whereas the National Government still looked strong. In May 1935 Baldwin had replaced the ailing MacDonald, whose mental powers had begun to fade with alarming rapidity and whose natural tendency towards indecision and misty generalization had turned almost to incoherence.

Clement Attlee led Labour into the general election as a stopgap leader, but there was no realistic chance of winning. He had no answer to Baldwin's jibe that Labour claimed to support the League of Nations and collective security, but consistently voted against the defence estimates. The fear that a Labour government would cause foreign investors to abandon Britain was still strong, carefully played on by the National Government. Baldwin could claim that his was the only party unequivocally committed to supporting Abyssinia and upholding the League of Nations covenant.

Labour won 154 seats against 432 for the National Government (which really meant the Conservatives) and twenty for the opposition Liberals. The newly elected government did not, of course, lift a finger to protect Abyssinia. Meanwhile Attlee, to the surprise of many, was elected Labour leader rather than Herbert Morrison. Bevan never thought highly of Attlee, as we will see, but Attlee was to lead the Labour Party for twenty years and was to give Bevan his best opportunity to change British history.

The Political Fortunes of War

Maybe it was 'the Labour Party or nothing,' as he told Jennie, but Bevan knew that by the mid-1930s most of the impetus for change came from outside the Party. The official party line was to treat Communists – and even the ILP – as lepers; and the Communists did not help by attacking Labour left-wingers and the ILP as the worst traitors to the working class.

Yet by 1936 the ILP, the Communist Party and the Socialist League were saying many of the same things and both the domestic and international situation seemed so dire and dangerous that most old tribal loyalties and hatreds had been abandoned. There was unemployment, on which their policies, if not their rhetoric, were much the same. There was rearmament – all three Left groups opposed it vehemently (while never quite squaring the circle between that policy and their wish to uphold League of Nations principles against the expansionist policies of Mussolini and, later, Hitler). Most of all, there was the Spanish Civil War (1936–1939).

With so much common ground and with disillusion about Labour's leaders so equally shared between them, it was hardly surprising that the Socialist League decided to start talks with the Communist Party and the ILP, which resulted in the launch of the Unity Campaign in January 1937.

Ernest Bevin was furious. His loathing of Communists could easily turn into loathing of anyone who co-operated with them in any way at all. The Socialist League was immediately disaffiliated from the Labour Party and the following month Labour's national executive decided that membership of the League should in future mean expulsion from the Party.

This was serious. It would mean mass expulsions, starting with Bevan and Cripps, who were convinced the Labour Party was the only hope for the working class. So instead they persuaded the Socialist League to dissolve. According to Michael Foot this was a clever tactical move to 'disperse the target', but it is hard to see it as anything but a climbdown – and anyway it did not work. Quite soon Labour's executive decreed that anyone appearing on platforms with Communists would be expelled.

The Left felt the loss of the Unity Campaign most strongly when it came to the question of Britain's attitude to the Spanish Civil War. In July 1936 General Franco issued his proclamation of revolt against the elected Republican government in Spain and a three-year civil war began. It was the first foreign policy issue on which Bevan had authoritative things to say. 'Should Spain become Fascist,' he told the House of Commons, 'as assuredly it will if the rebels succeed, then Britain's undisputed power in the Mediterranean is gone. We shall be too weak to offer any formidable resistance to the Fascist governments of Germany, Italy and Spain who will form an alliance.'

The Republic desperately needed weapons. Most of the Spanish army had deserted to General Franco, taking their weapons with them, and Franco was also being supplied by Hitler and Mussolini. But the British Government decided on a course of non-intervention, refusing to supply arms to either side – a course which suited Franco very well, for he already had arms as well as a regular supply of the most modern weapons in the world's two most formidable armouries.

Labour's leaders supported non-intervention. Ernest Bevin believed the issue was 'whether or not we would take a step which in our view would lead to war'. But Bevan and the Left went to the 1936 Labour Party conference in Edinburgh determined to try to defeat the policy. Bevan made a passionate appeal: 'Is it not obvious to everyone that if the arms continue to pour into the rebels in Spain, our Spanish comrades will be slaughtered by hundreds of thousands?' But the leadership carried the day.

He was horrified. Jennie wrote that when Bevan came out of the hall:

> ... he looked haggard and careworn. He looked as if
> he had just dragged himself from the torture chamber.
> And he was not the only delegate to feel like that. Out
> they came, singly and in groups, the most unhappy,
> guilty-looking collection of people I have ever seen.[17]

The Labour leadership changed its policy a few weeks later when it became clear that non-intervention was purely one-sided, but it remained the Government's policy. Spanish republicans struggled on for three bloodthirsty, bitter years to check the march of Fascism through their country, before Franco emerged victorious in 1939.

The demise of the Unity Campaign and the Socialist League left Bevan and Cripps without a political outlet for their growing frustration with what they saw as the Labour leadership's timidity and passivity. But the Unity Campaign had left in its wake one important weapon: a weekly newspaper.

In the same month that he began the campaign, Cripps financed the launch of a new left-wing political weekly magazine *Tribune*, for which Bevan wrote a weekly column signed simply 'MP'. His early pieces tell us the way he was feeling about the Labour Party. For instance, his unsuccessful bid for election to the shadow Cabinet in November 1937 prompted this outburst:

> Some of those the Party thought fit to elect to front
> bench positions are too old, and some of them are
> obviously too ill to perform their duties ... It is difficult
> to believe that the Parliamentary Labour Party
> seriously intends to fight for socialism when it selects
> leaders whose battles are obviously behind them.

Bevan was equally uncompromising about his colleagues. Cripps he always praised. Attlee he respected, but he made the common error of mistaking Attlee's self-effacing manner for lack of self-confidence. Morrison he thought, rightly, read too much statistical and political information and not enough of anything else, which made him 'a first class political craftsman,' but not much more. According to Bevan, Attlee's deputy Arthur Greenwood (1880–1954) was exhausted from making too many propaganda speeches. He did not say what he must have known (as did everyone in the House of Commons) that Greenwood was almost permanently drunk. Even Bevan preserved the niceties of the day: it was another two decades before the Press took to photographing inebriated politicians as they stumbled into their cars.

As for his leaders as a whole, Bevan was unsparing and despairing. 'It is the whole spirit of the leadership that is at fault,' he wrote in *Tribune*.

> It refuses to fight desperately and heroically on matters of big principle. It refuses to arouse the electorate on burning day-to-day issues, such as the Means Test, the forty-hour week, and Spain. It is too ready to compromise with existing conditions. It is too respectable and too statesmanlike: too frightened of offending the middle class.[18]

Many things were on Bevan's mind in those three years before the Second World War began, but two really touched his soul: unemployment and Spain.

Unemployment, because he knew what it was doing to his own people, the people whose lives he had hoped to improve by entering politics. Here he is, speaking on the Means Test in Parliament in 1936: 'I cannot move honourable Members to pity; it is impossible. There is only one thing left, and that is hate. I believe in hate more than pity, myself.'

Spain, not just because it was a conflict between Fascism on the one hand and socialism and democracy on the other

– as clear a conflict as Bevan could envisage between good and evil – but also because he loved Spain and the Spanish. He had holidayed there with Jennie, who wrote:

> If you live most of your years in a Scottish or Welsh colliery district, then one day find yourself breakfasting out of doors in January (in January, mark you) with orange groves around you, the Sierra Nevada on the skyline and a brilliant blue-green sea at your feet, you rediscover all your childhood's faith in miracles.

Apparently Bevan 'looked utterly at home in Andalusia'.[19] He went there again in January 1938 to talk to the soldiers and Republican generals. Ashamed that Britain had done nothing to help, he deluded himself that victory might still be theirs.

That was the year Hitler marched into Austria and, later, Czechoslovakia; the year in which the Prime Minister Neville Chamberlain returned from meeting Hitler in Munich with his piece of paper 'signed by Herr Hitler' and promising 'peace for our time'. There was no longer any talk on the Left of stopping rearmament, for the danger from Central Europe was now too clear for such talk to be credible. Politicians do not tend to admit to mistakes, but Bevan must have known he had been wrong about rearmament and Winston Churchill had been right. Spain was now what distinguished Bevan and the Left from Churchill and those in the Conservative Party who condemned the Chamberlain government's passivity in the face of Hitler's expansionism. To Churchill, Spain was an irrelevant sideshow at best – and at worst, Bevan suspected, there was a swell of support for Franco in the Conservative Party.

Labour's leaders had moved, too. Attlee's adroit, low-key campaign to change the Party's attitude to rearmament had succeeded (aided, of course, by events). He was also much more vigorous on Spain now. He had been there himself and had moved closer to Bevan's view. But Bevan and Cripps were still regarded as rebels because they advocated a united front with all those prepared to fight Hitler, including Conservatives of Churchill's persuasion.

It seemed odd that men who only a short time previously had been calling for unity with Communists now wanted to unite with Conservatives. It was also a little shameless to attack the Labour leadership for not taking the Fascist danger seriously enough so soon after opposing rearmament. Perhaps that was why Attlee, a mild-mannered man, was uncharacteristically furious. 'In 1939 as in 1931,' he wrote in the *Daily Herald*, 'I reply to those who ask me to change my faith because times are difficult that socialism is not a fancy fair-weather creed but a faith.' It was a neat way of turning the tables on those who argued that Attlee's leadership was insufficiently socialist. He even allowed the *Herald* to publish, anonymously, a pastiche he wrote of 'The Red Flag':

Then raise our pallid standard high
Wash out all trace of scarlet dye,
Let Liberals join and Tories too
And socialists of every hue.[20]

Labour's leadership took dissent on this issue very seriously. Cripps pressed the united front campaign after Labour had formally rejected the proposal and was expelled from the Party. Bevan protested: 'If every organized effort to change Party policy is to be described as an organized attack on the Party itself, then the rigidity imposed by Party discipline will soon change into rigor mortis.' But he and a fellow MP, George Strauss (1901–1974), were soon faced with an ultimatum. They must recant their support for the Popular Front within seven days or face expulsion along with Cripps.

On this issue the man who believed in the 'Labour Party or nothing' was prepared to be expelled. And so he was. He fell ill, depressed at his expulsion, but also about Spain, whose new Fascist government the Chamberlain government had rushed to formally recognize. Bevan and Jennie set off for a few days' rest at their Berkshire cottage and it was here, one Sunday in September 1939, that they heard Chamberlain's declaration of war on the wireless.

James Maxton and two ILP colleagues voted against the war, but Bevan and Cripps chose to rally behind the Government. 'Every good socialist will do his utmost to assist the anti-fascist forces,' they wrote in *Tribune*. But it was important not to 'permit the war to degenerate into a simple struggle between rival imperialisms.' The Labour Party needed to be vigilant to ensure that the war did not 'end with the purpose of defeating working class power.' And, foreshadowing the Beveridge Report and the 1945 Labour government, they added: 'It is already time to formulate the essentials of any future peace in the world, and the greatest of those is power for the working class to decide their own destiny in every country.' It followed from all this, of course, that Bevan looked forward to the day – which he rightly believed could not be far away – when Chamberlain fell and the war was prosecuted by an alliance which included socialists.

Attlee thought the revolt against Chamberlain should come from the Conservatives and that Labour could only watch and wait. Bevan grew impatient: the war was already being used to bring in Tory measures (the Government had taken power to limit wage rises, but not to limit profits) and there was no sign of a Conservative rebellion.

Nevertheless, Attlee understood the Conservative Party far better than Bevan. He knew that the slumbering giant had begun to stir. And so it did, to Bevan's great surprise, but not to Attlee's. Attlee knew precisely when to strike: he pushed the House of Commons debate on the British loss of Norway to Germany to a division, for his political instincts told him that the slow-brewing revolt on the Conservative benches was too big to be contained. And so it proved.

Attlee's political instincts again proved sounder when it came to creating a coalition government. He and Churchill both understood the damage that had been done in the First World War, when the creation of a coalition government was protracted by horse-trading over Cabinet seats and they were determined to prevent that from happening again. They quickly agreed an allocation of Cabinet places, Churchill particularly asking that Ernest Bevin should become Minister of Labour. In a statement signed by its entire editorial board (including Bevan), *Tribune* complained that Churchill had hoodwinked Attlee, cunningly appointing Ernest Bevin and Herbert Morrison to the two most unpopular jobs, Labour and Supply, and that Chamberlain and his allies had posts in Churchill's administration.

This complaint soon seemed trivial and irrelevant. In May and June 1940, the Fall of France left Britain fighting alone and facing the imminent threat of invasion. Bevan understood Churchill's value as a wartime leader, though he still complained that Churchill talked only of what was to be defeated and never of what sort of future people were fighting for. To understand Bevan's attitude we have to remember the end of the First World War in 1918: the cruel betrayal of the soldiers who were promised they would return to 'homes fit for heroes', but often came back instead to no homes at all and to the same unjust society they had known before. But if 1945 was not a repeat of 1918, it is partly because people like Aneurin Bevan risked unpopularity and political credibility by warning against it in 1940.

Bevan was perturbed by the personal ascendancy of Winston Churchill. Labour's leaders were all in the Cabinet and took collective responsibility, so they could not question Churchill in the House. Of course there had to be a Leader of the Opposition and in his autobiography Attlee is uncharacteristically frank about his choice: 'In making my recommendations to the Prime Minister (about posts in government) I had thought it necessary to leave out some of our older leaders. They were therefore available to lead the Party in the House.'[21] H B Lees-Smith (1878–1941)

– even then not a name to conjure with – became the official Leader of the Opposition and asked mostly undemanding questions of ministers.

Since nobody else was doing the job, Bevan appointed himself the real opposition leader, questioning, criticizing and reminding the British people that they still lived in a parliamentary democracy. With the Blitz causing mayhem throughout the winter of 1940–1941 and great swathes of Britain's cities being reduced to rubble, it was a thankless task that Bevan gave himself. At the time it brought him nothing but abuse, yet subsequent generations should be glad that someone with Bevan's ability and courage volunteered to do it.

He roundly condemned the Government for suppressing the Communist newspaper the *Daily Worker* and Labour leaders for stifling criticism of the Government at the party conference. After Hitler invaded the Soviet Union, Bevan was the first well-known politician to demand a second front, in June 1941. He shared the popular admiration for Churchill, but not the idea that Churchill was infallible and his attacks on the Prime Minister were often startling in their directness. 'A Prime Minister who is completely illiterate in all matters connected with industry, and who has come to think in terms of perorations and rounded verbiage' was how he referred to Churchill in *Tribune*.[22]

At the end of that year Bevan became acting editor of *Tribune*. The magazine was in financial difficulties and it was cheaper to have Bevan do the job than pay a full-time editor. Like most Tribune editors he wanted top-class journalism without the inconvenience of having to pay for it, though in a letter to Jennie he couched it in far more elevated terms: 'I shall edit the paper myself without salary, and I shall scour Fleet Street, giving journalists with good information and bad consciences the privilege of burning candles for their souls on the same financial terms as myself.'[23]

He persuaded the novelist George Orwell (1903–1950) to become literary editor and to write a regular column, a coup which brought in a few much-needed readers. Orwell, for his part, found Bevan a surprisingly good editor. 'Those who have worked with him in a journalistic capacity,' Orwell noted in an anonymous *Observer* profile in 1945, 'have remarked with pleasure and astonishment that here at last is a politician who knows that literature exists and will even hold up work for five minutes to discuss a point of style.' Bevan had what the Labour MP Denis Healey (1917–2015) has called the essential quality for a politician: a hinterland. He had cultural interests outside politics and that made his contributions inside politics much more valuable. Politicians who have no hinterland – Herbert Morrison is the best example among Bevan's contemporaries – become narrow and scheming.

The United States came into the war in December 1941 after the Japanese attacked Pearl Harbor. That same month the Red Army prevented the Germans from claiming Moscow. But the Americans would take time to come to Britain's aid and there was no guarantee that the Russian resistance could last. Jennie became directly involved with these events. After working briefly for Lord Beaverbrook at the Ministry for Aircraft Production, then as a columnist on the *Daily Mirror*, she was sent in the autumn of 1941 on a propaganda tour of the United States. The following year she wrote a short book of propaganda, *Russia, Our Ally*. Bevan's contribution was the best he thought an MP could make: he campaigned for Britain to open a second front in the East and ensure the Russians were not beaten. For if Russia were defeated and the Germans concentrated their whole force on Britain, how long could Britain withstand them?

The need for a second front was not Bevan's only complaint against the Government. He thought Churchill's very personal direction of the war effort resulted in bad decisions. The British army was riddled with old-fashioned British snobbery: had the fearsome German Field Marshal Rommel (1891–1944) served in the British army, quipped Bevan, he would still be a lowly sergeant. Bevan remained convinced that Labour's leaders were making a mistake by shackling themselves to the decisions of a predominantly Conservative government. He reserved the right to be strongly critical of Churchill and to rail against the growing hero-worship. He wanted much more nationalization to provide more efficiency in war production.

Bevan's main channel for all these ideas was *Tribune*. But at the start of July 1942, after Rommel recaptured Tobruk (a seaport in Libya, Northern Africa), some Conservative back- benchers moved a House of Commons motion of 'no confidence in the central direction of the war'. They did so, by general consent, incompetently, and if Bevan had not been involved the challenge would never have been taken seriously. In this debate he established himself as the only critic of the Government who mattered. From that day on, there was never any doubt he was among the two or three greatest House of Commons performers of his generation. The whole war strategy was wrong, he said. The wrong weapons had been produced and the men using them were not properly trained. He attacked Churchill, he attacked the army high command and he attacked the Government, including the leaders of his own party. Churchill, of course, won his vote of confidence overwhelmingly, but Bevan had turned it from a damp squib into a parliamentary occasion.

From that debate onwards the second front campaign could not be ignored. Nor could Bevan's increasingly personal and strident criticisms of Churchill. He ridiculed the Prime Minister's 'turgid, wordy, dull, prosaic, and almost invariably empty speeches.' He attacked him for wearing uniforms: 'I wish he would recognize that he is the civilian head of a civilian government.' He was furious at the way the Press had been bullied and censored into stifling criticism of the Government. He criticized the night bombing of German cities, which would no more subdue Germany than the Blitz had subdued Britain.

And on 9 September 1942 Bevan stepped over the precipice on which he had teetered throughout 1942: he called on Churchill to resign. 'The Prime Minister's continuation in office is a major national disaster' he told the House of Commons. Since he had no serious candidate to replace Churchill, it was little more than a piece of theatre. He did not suggest Attlee, for the Labour leader was now almost lost in Churchill's vast shadow. Attlee's influence in the dark corners of Whitehall was enormous, however, and Bevan would have been amazed had he known.

Bevan was roundly abused in the Press. 'These sour, snarling attacks must tend to destroy whatever status Mr Bevan may have acquired as an honest parliamentary critic,' opined the *News Chronicle*, while the *Western Mail* called his speech a 'disgraceful exhibition of peevishly offensive cussedness'.

Two months later, Field-Marshal Montgomery (1887–1976) defeated Rommel at El Alamein in North Africa. It was the turning-point of the war. It no longer made any sense to call for Churchill to be replaced, though Bevan did put the British victory into perspective. Montgomery, he said, had beaten fifteen Axis divisions, eleven of them Italian, while the Russians had for the past eighteen months faced 176 divisions. Weeks later, the Russians made further calls for a second front unnecessary by defeating the German army at Stalingrad. At last the defeat of Hitler looked not only possible but likely. It was time to turn to the question of what Britain was going to be like after this devastating showdown.

Throughout the Second World War Bevan retained his active social life and in particular his friendship with Lord Beaverbrook, whose appointment as Minister of Aircraft Production he warmly welcomed (unlike Attlee, who would have prevented it if he could). Bevan enjoyed splendid, alcohol-fuelled meals in the middle of the black-out with left-wing journalists – Claud Cockburn (1904–1981), Frank Owen and Michael Foot among others. He never stopped having fun.

Jennie and Bevan could not visit their country home as much as they had hoped so they reluctantly sold it and bought an eleven-year lease on 23 Cliveden Place, a Georgian terraced house near Sloane Square, London.

Sometime during the early war years, Jennie took another decision. She had been one of the first women to make a real difference in Britain politics and did not want to give it up. On the other hand, her husband had made an even greater impact, so she decided to subordinate her political career to his. She lived with that decision, right or wrong, until his death in 1960. 'She came during the war to realize that Nye's contribution to the Labour movement was far greater than anything she might contribute,' writes Jennie's biographer. 'Seven or eight years into their marriage, she found herself in love with her husband. The war not only made Nye the leader of the Left; it also made their marriage.'[24]

In the year 1942 Bevan and Jennie, along with the rest of Britain, could leave behind their daily fear of invasion. For Bevan, of course, there was a rough time in parliament to be endured, with no shortage of fellow MPs to say that while he sneered from the side lines, Churchill had been preparing for victory. As for his second front campaign, Conservative MP Commander Braithwaite seemed to have had the House's support when he asserted that soldiers regarded it with contempt and he got an easy laugh at Bevan's expense: 'I am authorized by certain ratings to say that they would be only too happy to provide facilities at the earliest possible moment for the member for Ebbw Vale to be landed on a hostile coast.'

Bevan's relations with the Party leadership were worse than ever. Attlee, he wrote in *Tribune*, 'is loyal to the point of self-effacement – but Mr Attlee is no longer the spokes-man of the movement which carried him from obscurity into the second position in the land ... He remains loyal, but only to Mr Churchill.'[25] In response Attlee observed in the House of Commons a few days later that Bevan 'is apt to become airborne in the last five minutes of his speech'.

In fact, Attlee's private criticisms had a far greater effect on Churchill than Bevan's public thunderings. Secretly, Attlee wrote a long letter to Churchill, mercilessly analys-ing the Prime Minister's 'method, or rather lack of method, of dealing with matters requiring Cabinet decisions'. He accused Churchill of never bothering to read papers or even the notes prepared for his guidance and when the matter came to Cabinet, 'not infrequently a phrase catches your eye which gives rise to a disquisition on an interesting point only slightly connected with the subject matter'. He also accused Churchill of being paranoid, imagining 'malevo-lent intrigues of socialist ministers who have beguiled their weak Conservative colleagues', which 'is unjust and insult-ing to ministers of both parties'.[26]

Bevan's one political friend in the Government was Stafford Cripps, for whom the war had brought extraor-dinary political advancement. Two overseas missions – to the Soviet Union and India – had brought him enormous prestige at home, though neither was a complete success. Cripps had also been placed in the War Cabinet, only to resign from it towards the end of 1942 because Churchill would not accept his proposals for overhauling the deci-sion-making process. He then took Beaverbrook's old job of Minister of Aircraft Production instead. To Bevan, Cripps's departure from the War Cabinet was a 'political assassination' by the Prime Minister. His *Tribune* analysis concludes that Churchill could not have got rid of Cripps without the renewed prestige resulting from victories in North Africa, which he used 'cynically, brutally and irresponsibly.'

This was rubbish. Churchill did not conspire against Cripps, who was under no pressure to resign. The truth is that, as Attlee once said of him, Cripps always thought the view he held at any given moment was the only view a sensible and honest person could arrive at – or, as Churchill put it more succinctly, seeing Cripps in the distance: 'There, but for the grace of God, goes God.'

Bevan was a lonely figure in 1942, railing against a Prime Minister who was fast becoming a national hero and always talking about the sort of society Britain was to have after the war, when victory was far from certain. Some of his attacks on Churchill and Attlee seemed over the top and often simply wrong – and appear even more so in retrospect. Yet we can now see that Bevan was the public manifestation of a growing determination among ordinary people and at the heart of government that this time, unlike 1918, the men at the front would not come home to the same injustices and hardships they had left behind. This time a new Britain would be created.

Four by-election defeats for the Government in 1942 convinced Bevan that the national mood was moving his way. Each by-election had been held in a Conservative seat and they had all been won by independent left-wing candidates – since the Labour Party could not put up candidates against a coalition government of which it was a part. (There was almost a fifth by-election defeat, which would have brought Jennie Lee back to parliament, but the Government unexpectedly held Bristol Central.) These defeats were a warning to the Conservatives of what would happen to them in 1945 and Bevan understood their true significance better than either Churchill or Attlee.

And all the time, right at the heart of government, a new Britain was growing and being shaped. The seed was planted quietly by Arthur Greenwood in June 1941, when he commissioned the austere academic economist Sir William Beveridge (1879–1963) to produce a report with the uninspiring title *On Social Insurance and Allied Services*. Beveridge took eighteen months to write his 200,000-word report and on its publication in December 1942 it was clearly a blueprint for a social revolution. The Beveridge Report, dry and academic though it was, was a surprise bestseller – a clear sign that Bevan's estimate of the popular mood was broadly correct.

Beveridge proposed a national scheme for the slaying of the 'five giants', which he identified as Want, Idleness, Disease, Squalor, and Ignorance. To achieve this he proposed a comprehensive welfare system including a free National Health Service, child allowances, and full employment.

The Beveridge Report was debated in February 1943. Churchill welcomed it with a phrase that has been ridiculed by the Thatcher generation, probably in the mistaken assumption it was coined by a socialist: 'We must establish national compulsory insurance for all classes for all purposes from the cradle to the grave.' It provoked a Labour rebellion, for Labour MPs could see that the coalition government was not going to implement the report: Churchill insisted that any question of implementation must wait until the war was won.

But while Bevan publicly accused Labour leaders of refusing to do anything about the Beveridge Report, Churchill grew increasingly mistrustful of his Labour colleagues, who he thought were trying to implement the report by stealth. Neither was right. Attlee, Greenwood and Ernest Bevin were not trying to subvert a coalition government for socialist purposes, as Churchill suspected. But neither were they trying to stifle the Beveridge Report, as Bevan thought.

In fact, Bevan's friend Lord Beaverbrook was the chief instrument Churchill used to try to ensure that Attlee, Ernest Bevin and Greenwood did not subvert his government for socialist ends. Beaverbrook and Brendan Bracken were placed on the committees on which Labour people sat to make sure they did not get up to any mischief. 'When they state their opinions,' Attlee wrote to Churchill, 'it is obvious that they do not know anything about it. Nevertheless an hour is consumed in listening to their opinions.'

The Labour rebellion was serious. When the overwhelming majority of Labour MPs voted for the immediate implementation of the Beveridge Report and against the Government. Wisely, Attlee did not attempt to discipline his dissident MPs and went on to obtain such advances as he could within the Government. Bevan continued to demand that Labour's leaders hold out for the full implementation of the report, even at the risk of breaking up the coalition. The time was near, he said, when the

Labour Party 'will have to abandon either its principles or its leaders.'

The country was with the rebels: a Gallup poll in July 1943 gave the Labour Party a twelve-point lead. Meanwhile, Attlee fretted that Bevan's antics could make the Party unelectable. 'A silly speech by someone like Aneurin Bevan might easily be used to stampede the electors from Labour,' he wrote in notes probably intended for a presentation to Labour's National Executive.[27]

Attlee's continued loyalty to Churchill irritated Bevan for the rest of the war but, despite everything he could do or say, the Labour Party did not withdraw from the coalition until after Germany's surrender. In retrospect, both men saw something the other missed. Attlee saw that loyalty to the coalition was not only the right way to win the war, but also the right way to gain the experience of government that would convince voters afterwards that Labour could govern. Bevan saw that Churchill's popularity as a wartime leader did not mean the people would vote for him after the war – the mood had turned decisively against the Conservative Party, which had given the nation the bitter hardships and inequalities of the 1930s.

In April 1944 the war between Bevan and the Party leaders came to a head when Ernest Bevin introduced a regulation imposing a penalty of up to five years' imprisonment for anyone taking part in an unofficial strike. Paradoxically, this brought Bevan into conflict with the unions, for Ernest Bevin's proposal gave trade union leaders the ability to legalize strikes, putting them in a position of power. That is why Bevan was able to say in Parliament: 'Do not let anyone on this side of the House think he [Ernest Bevin] is defending the trade unions; he is defending the trade union official.'

Bevan led a substantial Labour rebellion and Labour's National Executive Committee (NEC) demanded a written promise that he would toe the Party line in future or face expulsion. Bevan was in a quandary, because he stood an excellent chance of being elected to the NEC at that year's conference. He swallowed his pride and signed the undertaking.

> It is because I believe there are elements in the Party
> which wish to continue the association with the Tories
> when the war is over, that I refuse to allow myself to
> be manoeuvred out of the Party and thus leave them
> with a clear field to accomplish the ruin of the Labour
> movement.

And so, in December 1944, Bevan was for the first time elected to the National Executive as a constituency representative at a conference that had moved sharply to the Left and was ready to set out a post-war socialist settlement.

Bevan's attacks on Attlee became increasingly personal. Attlee had participated in the decision to send British troops to support the right-wing monarchist forces in Greece against the Communists. Worse, Attlee agreed to attend the San Francisco conference as deputy to the Conservative Anthony Eden. In *Tribune*, Bevan wrote:

> We did not expect that he would affront his own

followers and demean the status of the whole Labour movement by agreeing to serve as lieutenant to Anthony Eden. The whole affair is painful, humiliating and hurtful to the Labour Party ... [Attlee] seems determined to make a trumpet sound like a tin whistle.

Germany surrendered on 8 May 1945. The Labour leadership refused Churchill's proposal to continue the coalition until the defeat of Japan. The battle that Bevan had looked forward to so eagerly, and which he was certain the Labour Party would win, had finally begun.

Bevan Comes in from the Cold

The Labour Party would not exceed the scale of its 1945 landslide victory until 1997, when 'New Labour' took power, led by Tony Blair (b. 1952). But in 1997 the Conservative Prime Minister, John Major (b. 1943), was generally perceived as not being up to the job and his government had stumbled from crisis to crisis. In 1945, in contrast, the Labour Party faced a Conservative Party led by a national hero, Winston Churchill, whose popularity with the electorate was the Conservatives' strongest card.

The lines of the 1945 election were clearly drawn: on one side, the charismatic leader who had won the war, but who led a party that baulked at social reform and was associated with the Depression of the 1930s; on the other, the party which represented social change and a fairer society.

The British people were weary of war. Ration shortages and simple sleeplessness had eroded their will to defend the Home Front. Creeping to work through damaged and dimly lit streets, always doing without and making and mending, had created a desire for a different life in the future.

Since 1928 women over the age of twenty-one had been able to vote. They had borne the brunt of domestic hardship. They had died in industrial accidents, taken shift work and managed dangerous and dirty working conditions. Bevan, more than any other politician, was associated with social reforms that mattered most to women.

Only 60 per cent of those British soldiers who qualified used their vote, but those who did voted overwhelmingly for the Labour Party. Leah Manning's experience of being elected Labour MP for Epping is a good example. 'When the constituency boxes were opened I was well down,' she said. 'But when the soldiers' vote came to be counted, my pile crept up and up.'[28] The soldiers had seen the best and the worst of social conditions. Sergeant Teal was typical:

When we got to Holland we went to some nice houses in Nijmegen – flush toilets, nice gardens, they were just ordinary people, but so much better off than we were. I was flabbergasted. And when we got to Germany I thought, 'These people have been living well even under Adolf and I don't like Adolf.' I got ambitious. We owned two thirds of the world and we lived worse off than them.[29]

Dissatisfaction with social conditions was not confined to the army. The war was frequently perceived not just as a war against foreign enemies, but also a war to end the misery of the Depression. Some contemporary commentators saw it as a war against the confusion and backwardness of pre-war industrial development. Writing in Picture Post in 1941 Maxwell Fry had called for the damage done in the cities to be used as an opportunity to do away with slums and disease: 'The main roads of the country can be tree-lined parkways, even into Wigan – yes, and right through it … it is a hope that the mess of unplanned building and wretched advertisement will come to an end.'[30]

There had been a swing towards socialism as early as 1941. The war years had strengthened it, not caused it. People wanted a better life and they expected a clear programme of action from politicians to provide it. It was not worth sending the country's young men to fight and die if the survivors were to come back to a society where poverty, unemployment and squalor were common experiences and where there was little opportunity for ordinary people to build a secure and healthy life.

Older voters remembered the disappointment of returning from the First World War and the slide into the Depression. Women voters looked for a secure future for themselves and their families. Returning soldiers voted for a society that would reward their efforts. All of them were the people Bevan meant when he invited electors 'to bring to bear the same clarity of vision and doggedness of purpose which served all of us so well in the fight against the Nazis'.[31]

The Beveridge Report (1942) had become a focus for all these aspirations. Greeted as a call to arms for a better world, it had sold 100,000 copies within a month. There was a cheap edition for servicemen and women and in Occupied Europe it was distributed by the Resistance. It is probably the only government report to attract queues at booksellers. The Beveridge Report was not welcomed with open arms by the Government of the day, but commitment to it was part of the 1945 Labour manifesto: 'Let Us Face the Future.' Bevan had wanted the report introduced earlier, but now Beveridge's 'five giants' of Want, Idleness, Disease, Squalor, and Ignorance were to be vanquished in a post-war reconstruction that changed Britain for ever.

Prime Minister Clement Attlee's 1945 Labour government faced infrastructure and services that had been damaged by war or changed to serve the war effort and a populace tired of war and demanding change. Labour had promised a framework for change that was fundamental and far reaching and a political atmosphere in which socialism would provide a brighter future.

Many of Labour's new MPs were still in uniform. Others were unaccustomed to the respectability of being MPs for a mainstream party or had forgotten what it was like. Bevan and Stafford Cripps were back in the Labour Party – old quarrels, if not exactly forgiven and forgotten, at least not spoken of. So too was Bevan's old chum John Strachey and George Buchanan of the ILP. All four of them were to hold government office during the 1945 parliament. Even Jennie Lee was back, accepted into the Labour Party the previous year; though, as she wrote, 'It was not exactly an enthusiastic welcome.'[32]

Clement Attlee was not new to government. As an active member of the wartime coalition he understood the mechanics of power. So, for the most part, did his new Cabinet.

Forming the Cabinet was no sudden or unexpected task: as early as 1932 Attlee had sketched out initial plans for a small body of ministers and in 1937 in *The Labour Party in Perspective* he had emphasized the desirability of having ministers in charge of functions rather than departments. He made his first appointments extremely quickly because he had to have a Foreign Secretary to take to the Potsdam Conference with US President Harry S Truman (1884–1972) and Joseph Stalin (1879–1953) of the Soviet

Union. Potsdam would be vital in framing the alliances and economics of the post-war world. So Attlee wasted no time in appointing the first five members of his Cabinet. Herbert Morrison became Lord President and leader of the House of Commons and Ernest Bevin, rather unexpectedly, became Foreign Secretary. Hugh Dalton (1887–1962) could have expected to follow his interest in foreign policy, but instead was appointed Chancellor of the Exchequer. Arthur Greenwood (1880–1954) was appointed Lord Privy Seal and presided over social services activities. Sir William Jowett (1885–1957) became Lord Chancellor.

After the Potsdam Conference, nineteen new appointments were announced on 3 August 1945, though it was not immediately clear how many of them would hold Cabinet positions. All of them went to politicians who had served in the old Parliament and the average age of the Cabinet was over sixty.

If, as Bevan wrote in *Tribune*, 'the significance of the election is that British people have voted deliberately and consciously for a new world, both at home and abroad,' then new blood was needed. The new MPs were young, but the power was in old hands. It was not only voters who made this clear. When the House of Commons first met, Labour MPs celebrated by singing 'The Red Flag'. In stark contrast to the appointment of older men to government, two-thirds of the chamber were members for the first time. The surprise appointment was Bevan.

At forty-seven, he was the youngest member of the Cabinet. His record was consistent. He more than anyone else was the advocate of change on the Home Front. He had opposed the Government during the war years, but that opposition had been built on the need to introduce social change. Bevan's appointment was a clear signal from Attlee that this was exactly what he proposed to do. Bevan was the only minister without wartime government experience. The appointment, as Minister of Health and Housing, presented perhaps the biggest domestic challenge of the post-war government. It was not only Bevan's reputation at stake, but that of the Labour government itself as a force to change the future. At least if Bevan failed, it could be attributed to his relative youth and inexperience.

Lack of administrative experience did not hinder his instinctive understanding of the job – the ability to ask the right questions and the capacity to stand by his actions. Both briefs – health and housing – required determination, attention to detail and a grand plan. The socialist MP Barbara Castle (1910–2002) described Bevan as one of the few people in the Labour Party who believed that victory in 1945 was possible and who built that victory squarely on Beveridge's proposals for social reform.[33] Since Attlee wanted those reforms, Bevan was an obvious choice.

His appointment also solved a problem for the Prime Minister. The Labour manifesto had promised to separate the health and housing portfolios in the coming government. Attlee was now reluctant to take this step. It might require legislation, but it also meant adding another person either to his ministry or to his Cabinet. He had stated from the outset that he would prefer a small governing body. Attlee also saw ministerial responsibility as reflecting particular tasks rather than ministries and in post-war Britain the twin problems of poor housing and poor health were ideologically and practically linked. He had to accommodate those members of the Party and the wartime coalition who could expect reward and those ministers still responsible for fighting the war in the East. It was a bad time to add another department to the process of government.

Bevan saw both portfolios as part of the grand plan of socialism: to provide a better standard of living for every person. Some years later, in *In Place of Fear* (1952), he outlined the need for a free National Health Service by making a distinction between prevention and cure. He regarded preventative medicine as those social measures that provide sanitation, order and good living conditions and do away with the giant of squalor. Afterwards comes curative medicine, which provides for good health and attends to areas where disease appears.

In Bevan's view the 'whole' job should be done or no job at all. His vision took in both roles and bound them together. It is unlikely any other minister would have taken on these two distinct responsibilities with as much fervour as Bevan.

As well as attitude, Bevan brought another great strength to the Home-Front role: he could weigh up detailed arguments without losing sight of the grand plan. Ernest Bevin, who had no reason to speak well of Bevan, had spotted this while he was still Minister of Labour and National Service. Bevan was arguing a trade union case and as usual had come armed with both the rhetoric and the detail. Ernest Bevin was impressed. 'There's some stuffin' in that fellow,' he said. 'Me and him can do business.'[34]

For Bevan, even more than for his Cabinet colleagues, the task was to make detailed and visionary change, on a canvas reduced and rendered threadbare by the war effort and bomb damage. The British people were weary of the past, but had grand hopes for the future.

During the war years Bevan had engaged in grand, very public disagreements with every other member of Attlee's Cabinet. Now he was not only a Cabinet member, but a minister with a precise job to do. The success or failure of that commission would depend almost entirely on Bevan's ability to convince his old enemies that his ideas made sense. Attlee had quickly realized this. When he summoned Bevan to 10 Downing Street, he made it perfectly clear there was a clean slate between them. But would Bevan be able to bury old factions and disagreements? And even if he could, would other people let him?

Bevan believed wholeheartedly in the parliamentary process:

> Quite early in my studies it seemed to me that classic Marxism consistently understated the role of a political democracy with a fully developed franchise. This is the case, both subjectively, as it affects the attitude of the worker to his political responsibilities, and objectively, as it affects the possibilities of his attaining power by using the franchise and parliamentary methods.[35]

In 1945 it was not unusual to see socialism as the direct result of working class representation. Now, after almost fifty years of social democracy, the picture is less familiar. Lines are drawn between democratic socialism and the hard-line takeover by the working class seen as Communism. Years of Cold War and disillusion with Communist rule has hardened perception of a division between democracy and Communism that cannot be blurred. But Bevan regarded democratic socialism as a way of creating class equality and of eventually limiting the power of the capitalists; so to him, true socialism was a transition rather than a revolution. In the light of the events of the last fifty years, this appears to have been a false hope.

Bevan believed in parliamentary democracy as a means of transferring power from one class to another and he also believed that passing power to the working class would challenge the hegemony of capitalism. Provided they were given the social conditions to grow and develop, working-class people would cease to compete with one another and this new cooperation between ordinary people would come about through parliamentary socialism. So, in government for the first time, Bevan was already minded to do the job with his party, rather than against it.

It helped that he could present a detailed case. Ernest Bevin and Attlee appreciated a well-prepared argument and both men were often Bevan's allies. As Chancellor of the Exchequer, Hugh Dalton was the pathway to the necessary resources and it was these that dogged Bevan. Personally, both men shared a socialist vision and the ability to shout down a meeting and then go for a drink. Dalton's financial decisions reflected this and favoured Bevan when they could. For social regeneration, Dalton promised to find the money 'with a song in my heart'. There is a note passed between the two men at an early Cabinet meeting where they had disagreed and the Prime Minister had closed the debate. 'As half a real Welshman, born in Glamorgan, to a real half-Welshman, born in Monmouth, we must allow for these poor Saxons failing to understand our Celtic high spirits,' wrote Dalton. Bevan wrote back: 'As one bastard to another, I accept your apology.'[36]

This personal alliance may not have affected Dalton's spending choices, which were constrained by the economic climate of the time, but it did verge on friendship; and it went some way to easing Bevan's isolation in Cabinet.

Herbert Morrison was Leader of the House and Lord President of the Council and Deputy Prime Minister – 'A sort of informal boss of the Home Front,' said Dalton, 'interfering with everybody and everything.'[37] Furthermore, Morrison's way of working offended every one of Bevan's personal and political instincts. Morrison liked committees, he liked power, but worst of all, in Bevan's eyes, he seemed to like the idea of capitalist spending and organization. They argued about using private rather than state builders for hospitals, health centres and housing, and this argument, rooted in both practical and ideological considerations, came up again and again. Arguing with Morrison was a long, drawn-out process, as it had been during the war, and winning in one arena usually meant taking up the argument again in another committee.

Sir Stafford Cripps, now President of the Board of Trade, was the only real old friend Bevan had in the Government. But Cripps's function was peripheral to Bevan's brief and Cripps was also moving sharply to the Right in his political ideas. After 1947, as Chancellor of the Exchequer, Cripps's role became critical, but his influence on Bevan was small. Bevan was still bracketed with Emmanuel Shinwell as a troublesome left-winger, although this Cabinet was united in its drive to change Britain. Attlee, the quiet, temperate man, did not encourage alliances and in-fighting and this suited Bevan, who had a straightforward job to do.

Outside Parliament, Bevan avoided making strong alliances. His priority was the task ahead. Even Jennie could not count on his support and guidance in her role as a sometimes dissident back-bencher. Bevan was close to Michael Foot and to other old friends on *Tribune*, but he did not count on their influence on policy-making. He made no contact with the Keep Left group, while at home he enjoyed the company of non-politicians, and worked.

During his period in government Bevan changed the habits of a lifetime. Instead of working in the evening and at night and sleeping in the morning, he rose early, ate breakfast and went to the office. He came home at night and worked upstairs. Jennie kept track of his hours and would sometimes intervene with characteristic good humour. When he asked her to bring him a second brief-case late one night, she replied: 'No. One you may have, but taking two to bed is positively immoral.'38

Jennie's life had changed too. In 1945 she had returned to Parliament after an absence of fourteen years. She planned to continue her independent career, but was increasingly involved in supporting Bevan's endeavours. 'I reconciled myself to the strains because he was my alter ego,' she said later. 'We were never at any time conflicting egos. He was doing what I wanted done infinitely better than I could have done it.'[39]

This does not mean she had no influence on him – but it is true she had less patience with the compromises of high office. Bevan caused one of those little flutters of excitement that Westminster and the Press thrive on – then as now – when he arrived at a smart event wearing a lounge suit. Attlee took him to one side and quietly asked him to wear a dinner-jacket next time. Bevan regarded a dinner-jacket as the uniform of the ruling class, but he discussed it with Jennie and they agreed it was not worth fighting over, so he bought one. Afterwards, however, she met Violet Attlee in the House of Commons, who appeared so triumphant about Bevan's climbdown that Jennie went home furious and the dinner-jacket was never worn.

This is the sort of incident that Attlee probably had in mind when he observed of Bevan's relationship with Jennie: 'He needed a sedative. He got an irritant.' Jennie feared becoming the sort of political wife who merely influences her husband's wardrobe. It was the perfect role for someone like Violet Attlee, but Jennie was an active MP with a serious contribution to make to British politics. Later, when it came to the question of Bevan's resignation, she made sure her voice was heard.

In Cabinet, Bevan did not seek to make alliances or to continue old feuds. He was content to be a fairly youthful and inexperienced member. His job could not have suited him better had he picked it himself. In Parliament, he was happy to retain old friendships without becoming embroiled in party disputes. In his private life, he settled into a domestic routine that allowed him breaks from public responsibility.

It is hard to imagine the thoughts and feelings of this new Labour government as they confronted the monumental task before them. Their mandate was clear: to bring about a significant change in the lives of the ordinary people who had voted for them and never to return to the economic and social despair of the 1930s. Their blueprint was the Beveridge Report.

The problems were enormous and the huge electoral mandate the Party had achieved was, in itself, daunting. Britain was in an unprecedented state of disrepair. Soldiers were returning from the front, women were leaving their wartime jobs and both the social fabric and the economic infrastructure of the country had been driven by many years of warfare. War was still being fought on the Eastern front and the work of 'brokering' peace and reconstructing Europe had barely begun.

The historian Peter Hennessy captures the mood:

The appearance of ordinary people in the street would surprise you – pale faces, drab, often threadbare clothing with a sameness about it that came from rationing and standard Board of Trade approved designs. Men all seemed to be wearing the same suit of the classic de-mob type ... packed meetings of suddenly undeferential villagers applauded every expression of hope for a socialist Europe and every reference to the heroism of the European Resistance movements or the feats of the Red Army.[40]

British people had won the war – now they expected their reward. Britain could not be a poor country. In the wake of such victory, the working class did not expect poverty and want. Bevan understood what they wanted: 'It was about that home you and your girl have been dreaming about and writing to each other about.'[41]

But British hopes and aspirations were in danger of being torpedoed by the United States. Superficially, Britain was, with America and Russia, one of the three great super-powers. In reality she was the poorest of poor relations. And when, soon after the election, President Truman suddenly and unexpectedly ended Lend-Lease, it looked as if the British government would not be able to bring in the reforms expected of it; would not even be able to feed people.

Lend-Lease was the wartime arrangement by which Britain received US supplies on deferred payment. The decision that henceforth Britain must pay on the nail for everything supplied by the United States was taken so quickly and so unexpectedly that two ships about to leave New York had to turn around and come home.

The British government had to borrow money – and only the United States was in a position to lend it. Attlee sent the great economist John Maynard Keynes to Washington with his begging bowl, believing a loan on decent conditions could be obtained. But the men Keynes met in Washington were only interested in using Britain's plight to increase America's already huge economic and geopolitical power.

After months of negotiation, Keynes returned, not with the $5 billion Britain needed, but with $3.5 billion on harsh interest terms and, crucially, he had to agree to convertibility. Within a year of the loan being granted, Britain must make sterling convertible to dollars on demand. This was certain to lead to a run on the pound and a further economic crisis, which it duly did two years later. The terms of the loan made Britain a permanent economic vassal to the United States and set the tone for the relationship between the two countries which persists today.

Attlee, Morrison, Ernest Bevin, Dalton and Cripps were intimately concerned with the negotiation, but when the full Cabinet discussed the issue Shinwell and Bevan opposed the new agreement, seeing it as an American attempt to break up the sterling area. Bevan was reluctant to believe that Britain – 'an island almost made of coal and surrounded by fish' – could become dependant on dollars.[42] Shinwell argued that the American terms were incompatible with a planned socialist economy at home.

Nonetheless, the American conditions were accepted. Attlee maintained until his death that there had been no alternative: 'Our reserves were running out fast, we were as tough as we dared.'[43] The implications of the terms of the loan were key to the economic climate in which the Welfare State was built, but those implications were neither Bevan's doing, nor avoidable. He accepted this when he told the 1948 Labour Party conference that without Marshall Aid from America, on the only terms possible, Britain would have had one and a half million people unemployed.

Implications on the Home Front were barely less catastrophic. To make matters worse, the ravages of war came at the end of the long economic Depression of the 1930s and after a series of Conservative pre-war governments had severely limited public spending.

Britain was still one of the world's richer nations. Only neutral countries in Europe – and of course the United States and Canada – were in better shape. Britain's technological industries such as aircraft, electronics and vehicle manufacture were all well placed. Shipbuilding and cotton had done well during the war, but their position was contradictory – outdated machinery had been running at full productivity and now lagged behind America. And the armed forces must either be demobilized and returned to civilian life or retained in the military. Neither course of action was easy.

Bevan was responsible for the social framework of housing and health: preventative medicine in the form of clean and hygienic homes; curative medicine in the form of doctors and hospitals. All of which had to be built using an economy battered by war and undermined by loan repayments, and in the spirit of democratic socialism. The Welsh miner's son had his work cut out for him.

The Homes and Hospitals
that Nye Built

Bevan's first act on entering his ministry was to remove the large, soft leather chair. 'This won't do,' he said. 'It drains all the blood from the head and explains a lot about my predecessors.' He was a working minister, identifying closely with his civil servants. Bevan's Chief Medical Officer, Sir William Wilson Jameson (1885–1962), says Bevan 'sold himself to the ministry within a fortnight'. This was vital if the department was to work with him during the years ahead, but it was also part of Bevan's approach to the job. He saw himself as a member of the workforce. 'Never once during the 1945–1950 government,' said Jennie, 'did he come home and complain about his permanent officials. On the contrary, he was full of gratitude to them and was worried only by the strains he was imposing on them.'[44]

Bevan's next move was indicative of his ability to see the broader picture through detailed analysis. He prepared a questionnaire for officials to give him key funding information. The welfare situation he had inherited was a confusing patchwork. Pre-war voluntary and charitable provision had been combined and used during wartime with little overall plan or awareness. The situation Bevan had inherited was different to that which had inspired the Beveridge Report, but nobody knew exactly how different or where those differences were. When the questionnaire returns showed that between 70 and 90 per cent of funds were public, Bevan began to work on a management model that would reflect public interests.

The results of this process established both public housing and public health as national services. This model was – and still is – unique to Britain and the years after 1945. Bevan's model of preventative medicine in the form of good quality housing and curative medicine in the form of health services free to all at the point of delivery has never been repeated.

The Housing Act of 1946 consolidated subsidies and central funding for social housing, while the National Health Service Act established the National Health Service (NHS) from July 1948. Preparation for the parliamentary action and preparation for the services was not straightforward, however. It would be hard to imagine a modern-day minister preparing, writing and steering two such major bills through the house in the five-year life of a government, let alone in one year.

Bevan proceeded on two assumptions, which he clearly stated in 1944. 'The first consideration is to see to it that the dominant role in society is played by public ownership and freedom for the worker means freedom from poverty, insecurity and unemployment.'[45]

He believed that, given freedom from competition for resources, workers would and could build a democratic and fair society.

To provide this freedom in both housing and health, he needed to build on existing provision to make a cohesive plan. To do this, he must carry the dream and convince others of the detail. He had limited resources and his communications systems were fractured and war-oriented.

In 1945 the biggest issue on the British people's agenda was affordable homes. Bevan had included a whole chapter on housing strategy in *Why Not Trust The Tories?* (1944), because where and how to live after the war was every serviceman's worry – and dream. There was bomb damage everywhere and homeless and displaced people were visible in every town and city. In Britain 200,000 houses had been destroyed and perhaps another 250,000 so badly damaged they could not be lived in. No new homes had been built during the war, but the population had increased by a million. Naturally, pre-war Conservative spending on housing had been almost non-existent.

Bevan claimed he spent 'but five minutes a week on housing.' This cannot be true and it was certainly not what the doctors thought; they accused him of neglecting health for housing. Bevan knew exactly what he wanted and had already set out his intentions. He believed in planning, in space and in equity of access and public ownership. He built for the long term and was prepared to sacrifice quantity for quality. 'We shall be judged for a year or two by the numbers of houses we build,' he said. 'We shall be judged in ten years' time by the type of houses we build.'[46]

Although the NHS is always linked with Bevan, it was his housing policy that left the biggest mark on Britain's towns and cities. His were the big houses, built in groups and squares, just outside every major city centre. They had gardens, downstairs lavatories and 900 square feet of living space. No rabbit-hutches, these. They were the first houses

to be sold off by Margaret Thatcher's Conservative government (1979–90) and now they are at the forefront of the
property boom.

Bevan's housing policy took three paths. Initially there
had to be a 'make-do-and-mend' exercise to satisfy immediate need. Repair of houses and pre-fabricated houses were
only a short-term answer. Bevan hated post-war pre-fabs,
but the public did not. Many were still providing family
homes well into the 1990s.

Next there had to be new homes available for every
family. Bevan built a million houses before 1950, despite
scarce resources and a limited workforce. When the future
Labour Party leader Neil Kinnock was a child, his parents
moved to a new Bevan bungalow in Tredegar. Later he
described it as like 'moving to Beverley Hills.'[47] Thirdly,
there were to be new towns and villages built close to
jobs to reproduce a proper English village in which 'the
doctor, the grocer, the butcher and the farm labourer all
lived on the same street. I believe that is essential for the
full life of the citizen ... To see the living tapestry of a mixed
community.'[48] This last initiative revealed Bevan's intention
to destroy class barriers in British society. The new towns
were still building sites in 1951 and had not been part of the
1945 Labour Party manifesto, but they were an integral part
of the dream.

Central to the dream was public ownership. Council
housing was not new in 1945. The Housing of the Working
Classes Act (1885) was an early government attempt to
house poor people. The 1919 Housing and Town Planning
Act, under the government of David Lloyd George,

required local authorities to assess housing needs in their area and make plans to meet them. In 1924 the first Labour government gave local authorities the responsibility for providing houses, offering a subsidy on each house let and a long-term housing programme as ways of encouraging provision of working class homes. This act, the most successful inter-war housing act was drawn up by John Wheatley (David Bevan's political hero). By the time of its repeal in 1933, it had provided Britain's working class with 493,000 council houses.

Bevan learned from the shortcomings of the 1924 Act. Successful though it was, it did not lay down minimum space targets, only recommendations. By 1927 the housing manual was suggesting 180 square feet of living space and a separate parlour. As a result those 1930s council houses have much smaller living spaces and parlours that are little more than nooks opening from the living room. In Leeds, for instance, the big 1930s estates are now awash with builders providing conversions and extensions.

Central government would provide most of the funds for the dream, but the responsibility was local. In 1938, 13 per cent of housing was council owned; 60 per cent was privately rented. Wheatley's principle was to provide a government subsidy for each house let by the local authority. Although the amount changed, this meant that houses built by and let by the local authority attracted payment for up to forty years. That way, rents could be kept low.

Bevan's Housing (Financial and Miscellaneous Provisions) Act of 1946 built on these foundations. It increased and formalized subsidy arrangements to local authorities and it embedded space standards in law, not policy. It was the foundation of the post-war building programme – from just 1,000 houses and 10,000 pre-fabs by December 1945 (with 60,000 repairs), to 227,000 houses and 125,000 pre-fabs in 1948. All this in a country racked by debt with chronic shortages of materials and workers and where lack of fuel had reached crisis point.

Rather than rebuilding the structure, Bevan shifted the emphasis of provision. He used the local authorities as his organizing tool and central funding as a unifying force. Embedding house sizes in legislation ensured that housing would be of equal quality. Using local materials where possible, even if they were more expensive, was part of the dream of classless, affordable housing with no ghettos.

Bevan saw ghettos of the poor and ghettos of the elderly as equally undesirable. 'We don't want a country of East Ends and West Ends,' he said. 'Equally, I hope the old people will not be asked to live in colonies of their own – they do not want to look out of their windows on an endless procession of the funerals of their friends; they also want to look out at perambulators.'[49] Bevan saw that the ideal town or village would be populated with families. Husbands would be able to earn a wage and wives would have space enough and community support to bring up the children. The factory owner and the factory worker would live side by side. In 1948 he removed from the legislation the requirement for council housing to be solely for the 'working class'. In his view, housing should be provided solely on the basis of need.

His strategy was precise and integrated. He refused to

provide housing targets and was roundly criticized for it. His argument was that targets made governments build without standards or planning. Prime Minister Attlee would have preferred targets. Without them, he had no answer for the electorate for whom there would never be sufficient housing and no answer for the committees that saw resources poured into building without a concrete result. Forced to address this issue, Bevan undertook to provide monthly reports from 1945 to 1947.

He restricted private building for sale to a fifth of the total houses built. He rejected calls for a centralized body for housing in favour of local control of central funding. The New Towns Act (1946) and the Town and Country Planning Act (1947) embody the principle of planning in towns and cities. They were steered through Parliament by Lewis Silkin (1889–1972), Minister of Town and Country Planning, but they embody Bevan's principles of mixed, good quality housing available to all.

All of this supported Bevan's passionate belief that the dominant role in society should be played by public ownership and that freedom for the worker meant freedom from poverty, insecurity and unemployment.

Bevan dreamed of a socialist Britain in which good quality housing is cheap and affordable and in which class differences are reduced through proximity. On the contrary, modern housing is again in crisis with a chronic lack of affordable homes for key workers, ghetto estates and a marked geographical division between rich and poor.

Bevan's housing policy was part of his dream of a democratic socialist society. He never intended his houses to be short-term solutions and refused repeated calls to reduce standards in order to increase quantity, saying it was the coward's way out. 'If we wait a little longer,' he said, 'that will be far better than doing ugly things now and regretting them for the rest our lives.'[50]

The new National Health Service was to be realized in the same atmosphere of scant resources. This job was even harder. It was not only a case of politicking for building resources and standards. Bevan had to negotiate with one of the most powerful and the most conservative of post-war pressure groups: the British Medical Association.

He inherited a complex patchwork of voluntary, charitable and local hospitals and doctor's panels that had been streamlined rather than destroyed by the demands of war. The wartime Emergency Medical Service had used consultants for free in general hospitals as part of the demands of war. This was a new initiative and opened the door to the possibility of mixing paid and free provision. Many of the pay and contractual issues had already been debated. The pre-1945 Labour manifesto had been clear: provision of local hospitals should be the responsibility of municipal government (local authorities) and free at the point of delivery.

Bevan saw health provision as both an individual right and a social obligation. 'The collectivist principle asserts that the resources of medical skill and the apparatus of healing shall be placed at the disposal of the patient, without charge, when he or she needs them,' he wrote, adding that 'preventable pain is a blot on any society.' He gave careful thought to the funding of such a responsibility and rejected the idea of an insurance-based service. It would be difficult to give fair treatment to people with different qualification entitlements. 'Imagine a patient lying in hospital after an operation,' he said, 'and ruefully reflecting that if the operation had been delayed another month he would have qualified for the operation benefit.' Bevan also rejected a means-tested service on the grounds that it was immoral to refuse treatment to those who could not afford it. 'You can always "pass by on the other side"', he admitted. 'That may be sound economics'. 'It could not be worse morals.' But he was most critical of a system that provided different benefits for different people. 'The really objectionable feature is the creation of a two-standard health service, one below and one above the salt ... Even if the service given is the same in both categories there will always be a suspicion in the mind of the patient that it is not so, and this again is not a healthy mental state.'[51]

Hospitals were run by local authorities or by charitable organizations or they charged for their services. General practitioners were private and paid by patients or supported by the local authority or worked on a voluntary basis. Most doctors had private patients and 'panel' patients, with responsibility and control for a particular area. Specialist care was provided by consultants who were paid for their services either by individual patients or by donation. Dentists and opticians were private businesses.

These essential services were a hit-and-miss affair before 1945. The present authors grandmother used to keep a small amount of cash in a button tin in case one of her three daughters needed medical treatment. After 1945 she kept the tin as a reminder of the past and we played with the curious coins as children. Our grandmother had dozens of stories. Once, when all the children in the block of flats were ill with scarlet fever, the doctor had returned many times. Our grandmother quickly used up her little stock of coins and had to raid the children's piano-lesson money as well as their school fares.

Bevan was quick to make his first decision, which reflected his commitment. Within the first month of the new Labour government he rejected plans for local authority controlled hospitals. All hospitals should be nationalized, he insisted, and run by a central authority. It was the complete opposite of the strategy he had devised for housing, where local authorities were used for the provision and allocation of central funding. But Bevan took this decision in the light of two consistent and clear principles. First, health care should be free for everybody at the point of delivery. Second, if the state was responsible it must also be accountable and in a position to control.

Perhaps the biggest issue for the BMA was the way in which Bevan proposed to pay general practitioners, as the point of contact between people and health institutions. This was in the Labour Party manifesto and had been advocated by the Beveridge Report, but it was anathema to the BMA. Bevan proposed that family doctors should be paid a basic salary with capitation fees on top. This would reflect the numbers of patients in different practices and better reward doctors who saw more patients. The BMA complained it would turn doctors from freethinking professionals into salaried servants of central government.

One doctor was cheered to the rooftops at a BMA meeting for saying: 'This Bill is strongly suggestive of the Hitlerite regime now being destroyed in Germany.'[52] The debate between the Government and the BMA was as vitriolic as a similar discussion that arose many years later when the Thatcher government suggested that general practitioners (GPs) should prescribe from a restricted list of approved drugs. Bevan would have been pleased to see how much the BMA had changed by the 1980s: their contention was that prescription rules threatened not only their individual autonomy but the standards of care offered by the NHS.

In 1945 the intransigence of the BMA could have seriously delayed Health Service Day (5 July 1948), when services became free at the point of delivery. Bevan pushed forward his plans in the teeth of a majority vote from doctors rejecting the NHS.

The BMA probably misread Bevan's intentions. 'We not only desire this scheme to relieve patients of financial anxiety,' he told Parliament in February 1948, 'we desire to relieve the doctor of financial anxiety when he approaches his patients. It is one of the most deplorable features of the existing system that young doctors, when they go into practice ... have financial burdens put upon them.' Doctors would have to pay for consulting rooms or a position in a practice and for the necessary tools of their trade, before they were ever able to see a patient. Those with money could gain entry into a wealthy practice, but poorer doctors had to set themselves up in less well-off areas.

Eventually the row ended with a compromise that retained Bevan's basic principles: a service free to everyone at the point of delivery. GPs became independent contractors of services. They were self-employed and their practice was supported by the State. Bevan wrote the Act in a way that ruled out a fully salaried service and the BMA rank and file joined up.

A month after Health Service Day, a massive 97 per cent of the British public was signed up for treatment and only 10 per cent of doctors remained outside the scheme. These percentages remain more or less the same today. This partly reflects the lack of choice Bevan offered: it was obvious the NHS would go ahead and that there would be little or no provision for GPs who remained outside it. Joining under such circumstances was the line of least resistance. But it was also extremely popular.

This did not solve another BMA issue that cut across practical management and ideology. GPs owned their own practices and could therefore buy or sell a list of patients without reference to the patients' wishes. Doctors regarded it as a fundamental freedom to be able to choose where and for how long they worked. For Bevan, the fundamental issue was that people had the right to choose their own doctor. 'I have always regarded the sale and purchase of medical practice as an evil in itself,' he told the House of Commons. If doctors could buy and sell practices, the people were deprived of any choice. A related problem, providing services in poor or unpopular areas, was less of an issue in 1945 than it is today, when inequality and urbanization have created inner city areas with a chronic shortage of GPs. The BMA had provided some of the answers before Bevan arrived, agreeing to a Central Medical Board whose powers included suggesting to GPs where they might practise. This would be supplemented by the grouping of GPs in health centres.

In 1945, however, the main fear of GPs was that they would become salaried civil servants. Bevan denied this was his aim, repeating again and again that the Government had no intention of eroding professional autonomy. In *In Place of Fear* he argues that the collective principle must support the work of civil servants and that this in itself would create an altruistic service, but he did not follow this argument in placing GPs in the new NHS. The modern position is that general practices are controlled by the Family Practitioners' Committee and have been since 1948. The committee can prevent doctors from joining 'over-serviced' practices, but cannot force them into others.

The 1945 Labour Party manifesto had made it clear that health services should not simply provide cure for the sick, but should also offer health education and support. Health centres were at the heart of Bevan's plans, though his ministry did not see a single centre open. The idea was simple and went some way towards solving the problem of how to create a service that provided the same care in inner city areas and country villages, in better-off industrial estates and poor pockets of heavy unemployment. If GPs worked together in partnership their surgeries could be equipped to provide many more services than were possible in isolation. They could offer health care to the sick, but also act as a base for preventative health practices. But in post-war Britain the demand for new houses took priority over all other non-industrial building, so Bevan's health centres had to wait. In 1945 the provision of health centres looked like a minor issue among so many other pressing matters. In retrospect, it was probably Bevan's most enduring achievement.

In contrast, the compromise that has dogged the NHS since 1945 – and is still a political hot potato – was Bevan's treatment of consultants. This issue was central to his ideology: if the NHS was public and free at the point of delivery and delivered in the same way regardless of means, then the consultants stood to lose their lucrative private practices.

The consultants were not so easily coerced by offering 'no choice', as the GPs were. Unless there was some agreement, they would and could start a parallel health service offering paid treatment. Not only this, but there must be a way of ensuring that top-class consultants spent time in NHS hospitals rather than in their own clinics and practices.

Bevan's answer to this took two paths and was expensive (he himself said 'he stopped their mouths with gold'): he offered salaried connection with hospitals. Previously the association of consultants with hospitals had been, at best, an honorarium. Offering paid positions suited the hospital's needs, while framing the connection as a link with a hospital also defused the BMA's fears of a fully salaried service. Bevan also allowed consultants to use a proportion of beds in NHS hospitals for their own patients – a clever move that ensured the physical presence of surgeons and consultants in hospitals. On these terms, consultants supported the new NHS – which is just as well, because without them it would never have worked. At the time it was a massive coup for Bevan, although in later years it has created the biggest threat to his dream.

Bevan thought that demands on the NHS would reduce over time. He was mistaken. A healthier population has a higher expectation of health services. In the beginning, patients visited doctors and hospitals with health conditions that had been established for years. Today we are unlikely to suffer the damage of neglected and untreated illnesses that the pre-NHS generation suffered. In the early years of the NHS consultants described women coming in with prolapsed internal organs that had been like that for years and men with hernias and lung disease that had never been examined. In contrast, children born after 1945 went to the doctor with cuts and bruises, coughs and colds, and were treated. Many survived who would not have done so before. Most of us expect treatment when we feel we need it.

But as expectations rose, the population increased. Old people lived longer, babies had a higher survival rate and the medical profession got better at curing people. The first kidney transplant in 1964 was a medical breakthrough, but was immediately followed by demands for more. Critics of the NHS attributed this rise in demand to a blatant misuse of the service. Certainly, children whose teeth were treated between 1948 and 1955 – when dentists were paid by the filling – now suffer from a syndrome caused by the excessive drilling of milk teeth. There is also evidence of the misuse of prescribed drugs and of inappropriate demands on GPs' time. In the end, however, the twin pressure of an increasing population and improvements in technology are sufficient to explain the growth in demand – and expense – after 1945.

Bevan's new National Health Service began on schedule on 5 July 1948. For a little while it offered free treatment at point of delivery to every man, woman and child in Britain. It offered care regardless of wealth and position, as Bevan had promised. The NHS was in a position to carry out the dual functions of primary medical care in sickness and preventative health care, and continues to do so. (Health centres were not established until after 1950.) In the beginning the NHS ensured that some great consultants were present in public hospitals and that treatment for ill-health was a democratic right.

Like council housing, however, the NHS carried the seeds of its own destruction. Just as Bevan's quality houses were the first to suffer from privatization, so his negotiations to keep consultants on NHS wards are at the root of the re-growth of private hospitals. In fairness to Bevan, he could never have foreseen such dramatic reversals of fortune.

From Triumph to Resignation

On the appointed day – 5 July 1948 – five new Acts became operational. Bevan's National Health Service Act and Town and Country Planning Act were joined by the National Insurance and National Assistance Acts, giving a unified right to a minimum financial benefit to people who did not or could not work. Cover was 'from the cradle to the grave'; while the Children Act, providing for children cared for by the State, reinforced State responsibility.

All five Acts had been planned separately and took different routes to achieve their goals. Bevan's own plans for nationalizing the health service differed from his plans to develop housing through local authorities. Their combined effect was to introduce a new and very different approach to the welfare of individuals and the role of the State. For the first time outside Communist Russia, the welfare of the people was the responsibility of the Government.

The Acts were all based on the principal recommendations of the Beveridge Report and on the principle that it was the Government's task to defeat the giants of Want, Idleness, Disease, Squalor, and Ignorance. The agenda of shifting rights from the State to the individual was revolutionary. It was not an explosive break with the old order, however. Beveridge himself had been ambivalent about the radicalism of his proposals.

The provision for most of the many varieties of
need has already been made in Britain on a scale not
surpassed and hardly rivalled in any other country
in the world he said, and a revolutionary moment in
the world's history is a time for revolutions, not
for patching.[53]

This revolution was more of a re-framing than an
overthrowing or even a patching. It was neither socialism through the back door, as the Conservatives argued,
nor a mere sticking-plaster on the problem, as the Left
complained. During the war years Attlee, Greenwood and
Ernest Bevin had not tried to subvert the coalition government for socialist purposes, as Churchill assumed, or to
stifle the Beveridge Report, as Bevan thought. The post-war
'new order' was actually an attempt to solve old problems
and new demands. As *The Times* noted:

All parties in the State, as Mr Attlee rightly
emphasized, have borne their part in building up this
great structure ... For all their inevitable, and mostly
constructive, compromises, the new services attempt
to embody certain principles which today can be
fittingly recalled. They treat the individual as a citizen,
not as a 'pauper', an object of charity or a member of a
particular social class.[54]

For his part, Bevan did regard these changes as the start
of the inevitable rise of socialism. In *In Place of Fear* he
talks about:

... the dangerous period in the lifetime of a nation when the convictions, beliefs and values of one epoch are seen to be losing their vitality, and those of the new have not won universal acceptance.[55] But change was coming. In Europe the past is dead ... It was not Socialism that killed the capitalist competitive societies of Europe. They were killed by two world wars and by their failure to adapt themselves to the economic conditions brought about by their own agencies. At the moment they are floundering, unable to make up their minds which way to choose.[56]

This floundering, he wrote, would inevitably be brought to an end by parliamentary democratic socialism – 'based on the conviction that free men can use free institutions to solve the social and economic problems of the day, if they are given the chance to do so.'[57]

On the night before the carefully constructed launch of the five Acts to introduce the new Welfare State, Bevan made an important speech. His faith in a socialist future and his frustrated efforts to see Beveridge's proposals implemented during the war years led him to tackle the Conservatives head-on. 'So far as I am concerned,' he said, 'they are lower than vermin.'[58] This was hardly a surprise. In *Why Not Trust the Tories?* (1944) he had argued that the Conservative response to the Spanish Civil War proved that they were a serious threat to democracy. 'No,' he wrote, 'I don't think a Tory, considered as a person, is any worse or better than anyone else. But when you describe an individual as a Tory, you are saying he is a man plus something else.'[59] The something else was far from flattering: 'it was the ability to lead a blameless and moral private life while using subterfuge and lies in public office; because the Tory favours privilege over democracy.'

The 'vermin' tag stuck. 'It was, I think, singularly ill-timed,' said Attlee.[60] The quiet man had been building alliances and worried that Bevan's remarks would only increase public support for the doctors, who were still unhappy with Bevan's reassurances. It didn't, however, and Bevan was unrepentant. His view of the Tory Party was both emotional and rational, but he also feared the blurring of political boundaries. 'Then there is the disposition to smooth away the edges of policy in the hope of making it more attractive to doubtful supporters. It is better to risk a clear and definite rejection than to win uneasy followers by dexterous ambiguities.'[61]

On foundation day, parliamentary democracy irrevocably altered the balance of power between the State and the individual. The National Assistance Act and the National Health Service Act created nationalized schemes of support based on the rights of any and all individuals. While Bevan was clear about party alliance, the foundation of the Welfare State owes much to political consensus both before and after 1948. The breach in that consensus marked by Bevan's vermin speech had one vital implication more important even than Churchill's response or party trafficking: it undermined confidence in the new order. 'It is now possible to see the chief reason for our success,' wrote Bevan in 1952. 'It was self-confidence and the strength that comes from it.'[62] Without it the Labour Party was lost.

Bevan's vision of democratic socialism depended on specific economic factors, but the country was about to enter a worryingly unstable economic climate. Britain was deeply indebted – and at unfavourable terms – to America. It desperately needed industrial infrastructure and investment. Resources of all kinds were scarce. Both the NHS and the house-building programme needed money.

For Attlee, as for Bevan, these things had to be done, otherwise there was no point in having a Labour government. As the Prime Minister told the House of Commons:

> The question is asked: 'Can we afford it?'
> Supposing the answer is 'No,' what does that mean? It really means that the sum total of the goods produced and the services rendered by the people of this country is not sufficient to provide for all our people at all times, in sickness, in health, in youth and in age, the very modest standard of life that is represented by the sums of money set out in the Second Schedule to this [National Insurance] Bill. I cannot believe that our national productivity is so slow, that our willingness to work is so feeble or that we can submit to the world that the masses of our people must be condemned to penury.[63]

But resource issues dogged the Welfare State from the moment of its inception – and have done so ever since.

In Bevan's view, the working class would both contribute to and benefit from welfare resources. The people who benefited had also to be the people who, as taxpayers, contributed the money, 'otherwise communal need and private greed were in constant war with each other.' On the other hand, if resources were used by and financed by everyone, then they would be supported by everyone and high tax payers would willingly subsidize the poor. 'After all, what more pleasure can a millionaire have than to know his taxes will help the sick?'[64]

This might well have been the biggest mistake the miner's son from Tredegar ever made. He believed that, given free choice and economic security, people would work not only for their own good, but for the good of the whole population. It was this belief more than any other that was undermined by the Thatcher years. It depended on equality and on a vital connection between people. 'The capacity for emotional concern for individual life is the most significant quality of a civilized human being. It is not achieved when limited to people of a certain colour, race, religion, nation or class.'[65] Individual Tories were not excluded from this unified vision – except as members of the Tory Party!

Bevan, Attlee and the Labour government based their belief that resources would become available on two things: Keynesian economics and full employment. John Maynard Keynes proposed a closed system of economic management that was well suited to Bevan's ideals. He said that the manufacturer was the employer, but the employees were also the consumers of goods. If the consumers were well-off, they would buy more and the factory would be able to make more. If the factory made more, it could employ more people on higher wages. These people could then buy more – and so on, in a virtuous circle of productivity that benefited both workers and owners. But employers and employees are also taxpayers, so productivity made money available to the State as well. Therefore, the Government should put its energies into supporting industry or even nationalizing it. At the very least, it should put money into supporting wage deals and maintaining employment. Then, as clearly as night follows day, full employment would come, which would lead to less demand on welfare systems.

This is very far from the picture of a 'something-for-nothing' Welfare State, as presented during the Market Liberal years between 1979 and 1997. Bevan's Welfare State is driven by contributions from working people, given freely in recognition of the possibility of need or illness among their number. It is a sharing of the benefits of a productive State, where all citizens can contribute and have a right to the best the State can offer. Perhaps Tony Blair's view of a 'stakeholder economy' carries some overtones of this picture, where a stake in the economy includes the ability to benefit from services.

Bevan went further. He wanted to build a world in which there was time 'to break down the antagonisms between worker and management – time, patience and infinite ingenuity.'[66] A world in which working people were represented and enfranchised, not in an occasional parliamentary election, but in the multitude of everyday decisions that affected their lives. This could only be done hand in hand with public ownership. Bevan's housing programme had some of this – he used home-grown resources and labour whenever possible. And he saw the NHS not only as a service, but as an employer, as he told the House of

Commons: 'The redistributive aspect of the scheme was one which attracted me almost as much as the therapeutical.'

In his 'vermin' speech, Bevan went on to outline this view of democracy and power as the basic difference between Labour and Conservative: the Tories would always subvert democracy so that their own class retained power. And it was this political difference between Bevan and the Tories that was the issue of 1948.

With the base of the Welfare State secure, the Labour Party was planning its manifesto for the next election. The disputes that dogged this process were based in political philosophy and economic reality. Keynesian economics could not act fast enough to solve either the immediate or the long-term problems.

Between 1948 and 1950 there was little money and huge need. The winter of 1947 had seen freezing weather and vicious storms and fuel supplies broke down. In January1947, most of Britain was under six feet of snow, disrupting power supplies, stopping building programmes and halting industry. Even Big Ben was silenced, its mechanics frozen for most of the month. After the snow came the spring floods and after that the flu epidemic. This miserable legacy was carried over into 1948, which saw increased unemployment, industrial breakdown and unrest. The 'closed system' of Keynesian economics relied on continuous growth, but Britain's conditions did not allow for growth. They did, however, ensure massive demand for the fledgling services introduced in 1948.

At the same time, Britain was struggling to honour the US loan. It was the worst possible time for more expenditure and Bevan wanted the Government to concentrate on internal social services.

But Britain had been a world power and the Foreign Secretary, Ernest Bevin, was determined it should remain one. Foreign policy was formed on two principles: alliance with the United States and a potential threat from Russia.

Bevan supported neither of these. He saw America's free-market economy, with little restraint on the private sector, as a dangerous example to Britain. His own beliefs – increasing State ownership and responsibility and planning for redistributive economic growth – could not have been more different.

> Economic anarchy, the arbitrary decisions of the
> market place, are as senseless and oppressive to
> the worker in the factory as the edicts of political
> dictatorship. As for Russia: You cannot educate a man
> to be a trained technician inside a factory and ask
> him to accept the status of a political robot outside.

Bevan did not believe Russia was a serious threat to Western Europe, because it did not have sufficient economic resources. But that early cold warrior Ernest Bevin strongly disagreed and he, not Bevan, ran foreign policy.

On 21 June 1948 the *Empire Windrush* docked at Tilbury, bringing the first New Commonwealth immigrants. By the 1960s, black and Asian immigrants played a significant part in low-paid work and health-service care. But they did not usually benefit from Bevan's council houses, which local authorities let to 'long-term residents', until

1970s legislation made them change their allocation policy. Also, in November 1948, the United Kingdom proposed a Council of Europe, foreshadowing the development of the European Union. Keynesian economics only works (if it works at all) if there is a closed circuit consisting of workers, goods to be bought and industry. That relationship cannot be retained in a Europe without trade barriers.

To these economic troubles were added a forthcoming election and significant differences within the Cabinet. In 1948, Herbert Morrison announced the 'consolidation' of Labour's programme. It was, as Bevan realized at once, another way of saying: 'We're not going to go any further, at least for now.' The infant Welfare State was at least toddling and the programme for nationalization was accepted and moving, although not without setbacks.

Bevan saw consolidation as the biggest possible threat to progress. Socialism was coming and would come – but hesitating now only allowed space for mistakes and setbacks.

The conflict was especially harsh for his housing and national health projects. Where he wanted to be proceeding with confidence, building a new future and preparing a bold manifesto, he was having to fight long battles to retain even the two principles he had laid down: good quality, affordable housing for everybody and a quality NHS that was free at the point of delivery.

He had always refused to provide target figures for the numbers of houses built. In fact, 25,013 council houses were built in 1946 and a further 97,340 in 1947. In 1948 he built 190,368 council homes – 84 per cent of the country's entire house-building total. This was the high point.

'It was the only year in which the Economic Survey succeeded in forcing a projected figure on Bevan and he fell short by 49,632. It was not merely that site work stopped,' he told the Commons, 'the production of basic materials, such as cement, bricks and pipes, stopped. What is much more important ... was the diversion of a large number of building workers from the finishing stages of homes to the repair of houses damaged by floods and frost.'

Restrictions were on the way. On 1 August 1947 Bevan agreed to 'some reduction' in the number of houses built, in response to the need to keep sterling free for repayment of the US loan. In October 1947, 'some reduction' became an agreement for a limit of 140,000 houses. Bevan accepted this, but neglected to say that he had already amassed the raw materials for at least 100,000 houses. Instead, he asked for a reconsideration of the allotment in 1948. He managed to complete 165,946 council houses in 1949 and more than 160,000 in both 1950 and 1951. His total at the end of his five-year office gave council housing, run by and through local offices, 79 per cent of the total number of new houses in Britain.

It was still not enough to satisfy demand, but it was the high water mark of council building – not until 1959 did private building outstrip state building. Bevan's policy of granting licences to council house builders before private builders had paid off. New towns were also on the way – the principle established if not the houses built. Bevan could be forgiven for turning some of his attention elsewhere.

'Elsewhere' was the party programme of nationalization. Iron and steel were key to house-building. Nationalizing them was in the Labour Party manifesto and a vital part of Keynes's economic model. Public ownership was the next step to Bevan's 'democratic socialism' – to ensure that 'effective social and economic power passes from one order of society to another.' Not everyone in the Party agreed and progress was slow and laborious.

> It is a form of torture unknown to the ancients to be compelled on the last Wednesday of every month to convert the leaders of the Labour Party afresh to the most elementary principles of the Party. And now I can sympathize with that fellow Sisyphus and his bloody boulder.[67]

Steel was nationalized, but having won this battle Bevan found the NHS under threat. Initially there had been a huge demand for services, partly due to the snow, the floods and the flu epidemic of 1947 and partly, Bevan thought, a result of previous need and new interest. For whatever reason, the actual cost of the service exceeded the estimated cost by £91 million for the years 1948–1949 and a massive £134 million in 1949–1950. The obvious antidote was to pass on some of the cost, in one way or another, to the users of the service, but this was anathema to Bevan. He had enshrined his position in the first principle of the National Health Service Act: health services should be available to all and free at the point of delivery.

In October 1949 Prime Minister Attlee announced cuts of £140 million in capital spending and a further £120 million in current expenditure. This included a £35 million cut in housing expenditure and a proposal for a shilling charge on prescriptions issued by the NHS.

Bevan offered no public objection, but privately wrote to Attlee making it clear he expected the cuts to be matched by similar ones in defence spending.

> It, however, emerges in the final issue that the defence expenditure is only going to be cut on the administrative side, and even that in a full year to no more than £30 million out of something of the order of an expenditure of £800 million. When the two figures are put into juxtaposition, that is to say £40 to £50 million social services and £30 million on the already gorged and swollen defence estimates, I am afraid the result will be painful in the extreme.[68]

Painful not only to the socialist dream, but also possibly to Labour's chances in the forthcoming election.

Bevan knew that neither of these measures would be implemented immediately, if at all. He manoeuvred. Always a man who could see both the wider picture and a detail, he gave away the battle in the hope of winning the war. Much later, he admitted as much in his resignation speech to the House of Commons:

> The prescription charge I knew would never be made, because it was impractical. Well, it was never made. I will tell my honourable friends something else, too. There was another policy – there was a proposed reduction of 25,000 on the housing program, was there not? It was never made. It was necessary for me

at that time to use what everybody always said were
bad tactics upon my part – I had to manoeuvre and I
did manoeuvre and saved the 25,000 houses and the
prescription charges.

From the time of the 1948 Labour Party conference,
Labour's pre-election battle lines were drawn. Morrison
argued for the 'consolidation' of the nationalization process,
while Bevan wanted it broadened. Increasingly isolated
in his opposition to foreign policy and battling for more
domestic spending, Bevan wanted the electoral mandate
so that more progress could be made. The Prime Minister
set the date for a general election: 23 February 1950.

Thanks in part to Bevan's silence over prescription
charges and his success in providing good quality houses,
the Labour Party went into the election with a public
show of unity. But this was no re-run of the 1945 election,
even though the British public was once again faced with
a choice between Labour or the Conservatives, Clement
Attlee or Winston Churchill. Bevan campaigned hard, but
was dogged wherever he went by the 'vermin' remark. His
appearances became a whirl of Class War demonstrations
and heckling, hindered by poor publicity.

The Labour Party was returned to office, but with a
majority of only seven members. As Attlee is reported as
saying:

It must, however, be recognized that, with so small a
majority, there would be great difficulty in transacting
government business in the House of Commons. There

could, in particular, be no question of attempting to carry through any of the major controversial legislation which had been promised in the Party's election manifesto.[69]

It meant the end of Bevan's ambitious plans to expand nationalization and to build a democratic socialist society in which services were available and distributive and in which individual rights were afforded through State action and sanctioned by democracy. The best he could hope for was to retain what he already had: a working and still free National Health Service and an expanding, state-funded housing programme.

In 1951 he agreed to transfer from the Ministry of Health and Housing to the Ministry of Labour and National Service. It was not an easy move. His certainty that prescription charges would not be introduced had rested on an uneasy compromise between Stafford Cripps, the Chancellor of the Exchequer, Attlee and himself. Cripps would not impose the charges and Attlee would chair a weekly committee to consider NHS expenses.

But Bevan's old friend Cripps was a very ill man. In October 1950 he was forced to resign and died shortly afterwards. Attlee had only two possible candidates for Chancellor: Bevan or Hugh Gaitskell (1906–1963). The older men who had a stronger claim, Hugh Dalton and Herbert Morrison, said they did not want the job. They advised Attlee to appoint Gaitskell, who had worked at the Treasury under Cripps and had shouldered much of the burden in Cripps's last months there. Gaitskell got the job.

Bevan was furious. Partly because he had been passed over for a younger man with no roots in the Labour movement: a technocratic former public schoolboy. Partly it was because he knew that with Gaitskell at the Treasury the introduction of charges in the NHS could only be avoided by constant trench warfare. The Treasury was besieged by requests for money. Defence spending was rising alarmingly: British troops were fighting alongside the Americans in Korea and Attlee was under mounting US pressure to spend even more. Gaitskell was likely to support increased defence spending over spending on the NHS. The Cabinet was starting to look and feel old and tired, with Ernest Bevin also seriously ill.

The crunch moment came in April 1951 when Gaitskell imposed charges on dental and optical treatment in the NHS. Having publicly stated 'I will never be a member of a Government which makes charges on the National Health Service for the patient,' Bevan resigned.

His resignation, which set the scene for a decade and more of damaging internecine warfare in the Labour Party, looks in retrospect like a case of bad management. No one wanted it to happen, with the possible exception of Gaitskell. Attlee tried hard to find a way to avoid it, but he was working from a hospital bed while recovering from a serious operation and lacked his usual authority and sure-footedness. Ernest Bevin died in the middle of the crisis, at the moment when his old friend Attlee most needed him. Bevan might have stayed if Gaitskell had agreed to offer him a fig leaf by not setting a date for the introduction of charges, as Cripps had done. But Gaitskell, encouraged by the Party's deputy leader Herbert Morrison, was immovable. 'Nye should have been given more time,' observed Attlee many years later. 'Morrison and Gaitskell should not have dug in.'[70] But it was not to be. With Bevan went two of the youngest and brightest members of the government, Harold Wilson (1916–1995) and John Freeman (1915–2014).

Bevan used his resignation speech to make it absolutely clear to the country that the Government had invested in rearmament instead of welfare services. He also expressed regret at having compromised on prescription charges. 'I have been accused of having agreed to a charge on prescriptions. That shows the danger of compromise.' In the end, though, he reaffirmed an old faith, the faith at the centre of everything he had ever done in politics: 'There is only one hope for mankind – and that is democratic socialism. There is only one party in Great Britain which can do it – and that is the Labour Party.'

And so Bevan's only period of office came to an end. He remained on the back-benches for the life of that parliament, but the Labour government could not hold on for long with its wafer-thin majority. In 1951 Winston Churchill was returned to power. It was the unfairest result in British political history. Labour actually got more votes than the Conservatives – more than the total cast for any political party in British history. But these votes were polled in safe Labour seats. They simply piled up, uselessly, in the majorities of Labour candidates who were going to get elected anyway.

Bevan has often been blamed for exposing splits in the

Party that festered and kept it from office for the next thirteen years. What is certain is that he never intended to do that. The Labour Party was not just his best hope for democratic socialism, it was his only hope. His critics point out that the NHS charges over which he resigned were unimportant in the grand plan. There were already some small charges in parts of the NHS and he had remained silent over prescription charges. But right from the start of his office Bevan's principle of free delivery of health services had been fundamental, well-argued and clear. It would have been very hard for him to back down. Resigning, leaving a job, admitting defeat, making a stand, all depend on a split-second decision. Bevan made his without Ernest Bevin, who had died, or Attlee, who was ill. It is certain that he lost his temper and that he tried to avoid the final confrontation. In the end, however, Bevan resigned because health services should be free and this principle was more important to him than the Party.

Bevan and the Bevanites

Six months after Aneurin Bevan went into opposition, his party followed him there. Nevertheless, Labour leaders remained cheerful after losing the 1951 election. It was a narrow defeat and a moral victory: the only general election of the twentieth century in which the biased British electoral system handed victory to the Party with fewer votes. Attlee and his ministers were confident they would soon be back in power. Little did they know that it was the beginning of thirteen years of Conservative rule.

With more time on his hands than he had known for many years, Bevan wrote a book about his political philosophy, *In Place of Fear*, which he had been planning for some time.

One might expect a fifty-three-year-old politician who had achieved a massive amount of what he had gone into politics to achieve to be fairly cheerful, but Bevan was only partly satisfied. He felt the Labour Party slipping away from him again. The principal figure on the Right of the Party, Herbert Morrison, wanted an end to any talk of greater equality and especially of more nationalization. As one commentator put it: 'The Right thought that Nye had frightened the voters, the Left that Morrison and company had failed to inspire them.'[71]

Jennie was always less inclined than her husband to give the Party leadership the benefit of the doubt and regarded

Bevan as the leader of the Labour Left. Although she was proud of his achievements, she had never been entirely happy watching him make the inevitable compromises that a Cabinet seat requires. Bevan, on the other hand, was a practical politician who wanted power above everything else – the power to change society.

Soon after the election, at the 1951 Labour conference in Scarborough, Bevan had proof that the Party's grass roots were behind him. He was re-elected to the National Executive by the constituency Labour parties with an increased majority – and his supporters were elected to join him there: Barbara Castle in second place and Ian Mikardo (1908–1993) and Tom Driberg (1905–1976) with increased votes.

That very week, the three most powerful trade union leaders in Britain organized a Stop Bevan campaign. The most significant figure was Arthur Deakin (1890–1955), Ernest Bevin's successor as leader of the country's biggest trade union, the TGWU. Ranged alongside him were Tom Williamson of the General and Municipal Workers Union and William Lawther (1889–1976), the leader of Bevan's own union and miners' general secretary.

Between them they could control the Labour conference. There was no hope of getting a policy adopted if Deakin, Williamson and Lawther used their block votes to stop it. There was almost no way to get elected to the National Executive without their support. The only Achilles' heel in the constitution was the one Bevan and the Bevanites had used to get elected for years. In 1937 it had been agreed that the constituency parties could elect seven representatives on to the National Executive, instead of them being effectively chosen by the block vote of the unions. On these elections alone, the union block vote had no say. But if the constituency parties were going to use this power irresponsibly by electing Bevanites, Deakin decided, the 1937 concession would need to be revised.

The next annual conference in Morecambe in 1952 only confirmed the fact that the rank-and-file members of the Labour Party supported Bevan and the Bevanites – even if the big union leaders did not. Once again, and even more emphatically than in Scarborough, the delegates from the constituencies used their places on the National Executive to ensure a Bevanite presence. They gave the Bevanites six out of the seven seats. Bevan came first, then Barbara Castle, Tom Driberg and Ian Mikardo again increased their votes and Harold Wilson and Richard Crossman (1907–1974) were elected to the executive for the first time. Incredibly, they ousted the Party's great figures, Herbert Morrison and Hugh Dalton, as well as the Right's young standard-bearer Hugh Gaitskell, who was standing for the first time and who received fewer than half as many votes as Crossman.

What on earth was going on? Gaitskell thought it was a Communist plot. 'I was told by some observers that about one-sixth of the constituency party delegates appeared to be Communist or Communist-inspired,' he said in a widely reported speech after the conference. His unnamed source was a journalist on the *News Chronicle* – and he was wrong. Communists no longer had either the desire or the man-power to infiltrate the Labour Party. 'It is time to end the attempt at mob rule by a group of frustrated journalists,' Gaitskell added, 'and restore the authority and leadership of the solid, sound, sensible majority of the movement.'

With one speech he had established himself as the man the unions wanted. Deakin was frustrated at Attlee's refusal to turn on the Bevanites with sufficient savagery. Now he had found a politician he could do business with.

By the end of the conference the candidates for Attlee's successor were obvious. It was Bevan versus Gaitskell. And it was not only their policies that divided them, it was their style. One of Gaitskell's biographers puts it rather well: 'The Bevanites were a drunken night in Soho at the Gay Hussar ... The Gaitskellites ... were a night dancing at the Café Royal.'[72]

Churchill's new Conservative government did leave Labour's achievements alone for the most part. The NHS could not be demolished without courting electoral disaster. Council houses continued to be built, unemployment benefit continued to be paid and coal mines, railways, electricity, atomic energy, inland waterways, the Bank of England and the two major airlines– British European Airways (BEA) and the British Overseas Airways Corporation (BOAC) – remained in public hands. Only road haulage and steel were denationalized, partly because both were profitable. The trade unions remained a formidable force in the land and were treated with as much respect by Prime Minister Churchill as they had been by Attlee. What became known as the post-war Attlee settlement remained essentially undisturbed right up to the election of Margaret Thatcher in 1979. The economic policy pursued by the

Conservative Chancellor of the Exchequer Rab Butler (1902–1982) was so similar to that of his Labour shadow Hugh Gaitskell that the *Economist* in February 1954 labelled it 'Butskellism' and the name stuck.

This had the unfortunate effect of leaving Labour free to concentrate on its internal disputes. After Morecambe, the Bevanites formed their own parliamentary group, which met regularly every Monday afternoon under the chairmanship, at first, of one of the youngest of their number, Harold Wilson. This group was ferociously attacked as 'a party within a party' and was eventually forced to stop meeting. Nevertheless, a smaller group of Bevanites used the weekly *Tribune* editorial meetings as a way of getting together, until they started meeting on Tuesdays for lunch at Richard Crossman's house. This small group, many of them journalists by trade, included Driberg, Mikardo, Castle, Wilson, Jennie Lee, Michael Foot and John Freeman (1915–2014).

The Bevanites were never the sinister left-wing caucus with their own whips and discipline that Gaitskell and some right-wing newspapers thought they were. They lacked the ruthlessness or sectarian intolerance of the Bennites of the 1970s or the ideological purity of James Maxton and the Independent Labour Party in the 1920s and 1930s. Partly this reflected Bevan's own nature. He was no keener to be a rebel in the 1950s than he had been in the 1930s or the 1940s. Unlike Jennie Lee or Maxton or Crossman or Tony Benn, Bevan was by nature a practical politician who still believed that it was 'the Labour Party or nothing.' In fact Bevan was, as Crossman put it, 'a somewhat reluctant Bevanite'.[73]

Bevan was easily the most effective Labour speaker in

the House of Commons. 'When he speaks in the House,' Dalton wrote in his diary, 'he exercises a hypnotic influence over many of our people. It's pathetic and dangerous to watch their eyes fixed on him.'[74] Bevan could hold Parliament spellbound like no one else and drew huge audiences when he spoke in public. But these performances were interspersed with bad-tempered shadow Cabinet meetings. At one of these, Bevan and Morrison had a furious row about which of them had lost Labour more votes at the last election. Gaitskell believed it was all a plot to install Bevan as the leader of the Party to replace the ageing Attlee – the Party leadership was understandably much on Gaitskell's mind.

Bevan derided the house-building programme of the Conservative Minister of Housing Harold Macmillan, for Macmillan was doing things Bevan had refused to do. He was building smaller and cheaper houses to boost the numbers; to finance this he was starving other forms of building, such as schools, of precious resources; and he was relying on private firms instead of local authorities, so homes were being built where they were profitable rather than where they were needed. Bevan also watched Tory health ministers like a hawk, sometimes seeing threats to his NHS which were not really there or at least not substantial.

Bevan put forward policy proposals to go into the next Labour Party manifesto. He wanted a programme of further nationalization to include chemicals, aircraft production, heavy engineering and machine tools, as well as land nationalization. His proposals were usually voted down by fourteen votes to six on the National Executive

– just as the six Bevanites voted together, so did the trade union representatives led by Deakin.

Of the many issues that divided Bevan from the Party leaders, the most important was defence expenditure. It was really a rerun of the battle Bevan had had in Cabinet when Labour was in power. Labour's leaders wanted to support the Conservatives' defence spending proposals, which were not much different from Labour's own when in government. But Bevan led fifty-seven Labour MPs in a rebellion against them. He outlined his views in a series of articles in *Tribune* in 1953, which he called *In Place of the Cold War*. The causes of the Cold War, he said, were more complicated than just the perfidy and evil of the Soviet Union – and the United States and its allies ought to lower the temperature. That year he travelled widely, visiting India, Burma, Pakistan, Israel, Italy, Yugoslavia and Egypt and the following year he spent an instructive five weeks with a Labour Party delegation in the Soviet Union.

Abroad and at his country home with Jennie, Bevan was his old self, but in London it was another story. He felt increasingly isolated and unhappy and was prone to ferocious – sometimes alcohol-fuelled – outbursts. He was in a minority of one in the shadow Cabinet and was the leader of a minority of six on the National Executive. However, the burden of the shadow Cabinet was suddenly and unexpectedly lifted from him. In the House of Commons he listened to a speech from the Foreign Secretary Anthony Eden (1897–1977) which opened up the possibility that the United States might send troops to fight the Communists under Ho Chi Minh (1892–1969) in Vietnam and that

Britain might well send troops in support. Attlee did not seem to rule this out and a furious Bevan rose to denounce the whole idea in the bitterest possible terms.

That week in *Tribune* he spelled out his view in an article headlined 'AMERICA MUST BE TOLD: you go it alone'. Bevan had undermined the Labour Party leader and had to resign from the shadow Cabinet.

Harold Wilson had been the runner-up in the shadow Cabinet elections and was offered the place vacated by Bevan. Bevan assumed Wilson would not accept it under the circumstances, but Wilson took the view that since Bevan had not consulted the group before his action, he was released from all obligation towards Bevan and took the vacant shadow Cabinet seat.

At that year's conference in Scarborough the death of Arthur Greenwood led to an election for the post of Labour Party treasurer. Arthur Deakin had the necessary union votes sewn up for Hugh Gaitskell, but Bevan decided to make a challenge. He would no doubt be defeated, but at last union members would see that votes were being cast in their name merely to bolster the political careers of a couple of right-wing union leaders.

The election for treasurer was widely seen as a curtain-raiser to the leadership election, which could not be delayed any longer as Attlee was now seventy-one. Bevan's inevitable defeat left him, for the first time since the war, without a seat on Labour's National Executive, because a candidate for treasurer cannot also stand for the Executive. However, as usual the Bevanites made a clean sweep of the constituency seats, with Harold Wilson coming top.

Of real significance for the future was Gaitskell's victory as treasurer, by a wider margin than expected, but the conference is remembered chiefly for a phrase of Bevan's. Attlee had warned of 'emotionalism' in foreign affairs. At the *Tribune* rally Bevan had responded: 'I know now that the right kind of leader for the Labour Party is a desiccated calculating machine.' Most people assumed it was a dig at Gaitskell, but Michael Foot insists it was not. 'Of course I wasn't referring to Hugh Gaitskell,' Bevan once told him. 'For one thing Hugh is not desiccated – he's highly emotional. And you could hardly call him a calculating machine – because he was three millions out on the defence estimates.'[75]

So who was the target? Was Bevan merely describing a certain sort of leader, without anyone in mind? Or was his real target Attlee? What Attlee thought, we will never know. We do know that, when Deakin responded with a demand for Bevan's expulsion from the Party ('We'll have him out in six months'), Attlee was quietly determined to do no such thing.

The following year, 1955, the Government announced that Britain was to develop its own hydrogen bomb. Many of the Bevanites – Mikardo, Driberg, Castle, Foot, Jennie Lee – were unalterably opposed to this. Others – such as Crossman, Wilson and Freeman – were happy to see Britain develop a bomb, provided it was in the context of an East-West rapprochement that ensured it was never used. Bevan had been part of the 1945 Cabinet that had developed the atom bomb and although a hydrogen bomb was more powerful, there was no difference in principle.

The shadow Cabinet tried to fudge the issue with an amendment in Parliament that did not specifically endorse the bomb, but did not condemn it either. Bevan was at a loss which way to jump, but he could not ignore the views of his wife. At home Jennie would persuade him that the Labour leadership's position must be opposed, but back in London Crossman would persuade him otherwise. In the debate, he threw his dilemma back at his own Party's leaders:

Do they mean that nuclear weapons will be used with the support of the British labour movement against any sort of aggression? I want to know the answer. If my Right Honourable Friend the Leader of the Opposition says that that is the interpretation of the amendment, then I do not propose to vote for it this evening.

He did not get the assurance he wanted and in the end he and sixty-two other Labour members abstained in the vote. But the Bevanites were split and several of them, including Crossman, Wilson and Freeman, voted for the amendment.

Bevan had challenged his leader's authority on the floor of the House and the voices demanding his expulsion, led by Deakin, now became loud and raucous. Attlee, however, was determined not to hear them, as he had been when Bevan led fifty-seven rebels against him over the defence estimates. Attlee's handling of the crisis was the last great service this modest, quiet, deceptively adroit man rendered to his Party.

Gaitskell went to see Attlee to try to stiffen his resolve to go for Bevan's expulsion – and got his head bitten off. Deakin threatened to withhold his union's money at the next general election unless Bevan was expelled. At the Executive meeting, Attlee doodled on his pad while angry voices around him demanded expulsion. Then, without telling anyone, he went to see Bevan and agreed a vague statement of good intent, which he presented to the next meeting. Morrison, Gaitskell and Deakin fought a bitter rear guard action to get Bevan expelled, but Attlee narrowly prevailed and the Executive accepted Bevan's statement, with even less grace than they showed Jennie Lee when she was readmitted to the Party in 1944.

Attlee had patched his party together just in time to face the electorate in the spring of 1955, but it was a rush job. The British people were not fooled and returned a Conservative government under a new Prime Minister, Anthony Eden.

Attlee would have liked to retire after the election, but he was determined to leave the Labour Party in the best possible condition. He knew that a leadership election with tempers running so high could be extremely damaging. At any rate, if he left too early he might be succeeded by Herbert Morrison, which he thought would be disastrous. Attlee had at one stage hoped to be succeeded by Bevan, for he always believed the Labour Party should be led from the Left rather than the Right. But by 1955 he believed that Bevan's behaviour had made that impossible. This left Hugh Gaitskell, and Attlee did not think he was ready yet.

As soon as the new Parliament met, Attlee found the shadow Cabinet and his MPs urging him to stay. The most fervent pleas came from Bevan, who knew that a Morrison leadership would mean his expulsion from the Labour

Party. Morrison and Deakin wanted Attlee to retire at once. Morrison went so far as to get a round robin signed by a few supporters urging Attlee to do so, which Attlee serenely ignored.

But later that year, after Gaitskell's rousing performance at the annual conference, Attlee judged that he was finally ready for the leadership and promptly informed the chief whip, Herbert Bowden (1905– 1984), that he was about to resign. 'Shall I tell the contenders?' asked Bowden. 'Tell Gaitskell,' said Attlee crisply. When Labour MPs were called upon to vote for a new leader, the result was: Gaitskell 157, Bevan seventy, Morrison forty.

Of course, Gaitskell thought Bevan's extremism had cost Labour the 1955 election, while Bevan believed the culprit was Labour's anaemic manifesto, which he described as 'cold porridge strained through a blanket.' But at some level, both men knew that disunity was a more probable cause. The Bevanites were falling apart. Journalist Richard Crossman, who had moved from the *New Statesman* to the *Daily Mirror*, defected to Gaitskell. Harold Wilson was starting to establish himself as the leader of the centre Left, willing and anxious to come to an accommodation with the Gaitskellites. Bevan decided to do the same: he accepted Gaitskell's offer to make him the Party's spokesman on the colonies (Gaitskell refused to give him the Foreign Office brief he wanted). Bevan knew little about the subject when he started, but he learned quickly and saw faster than many the need, in a democratic age, for the colonies to move swiftly towards real self-government. He stood for the key post of Labour Party treasurer and the work of his supporters at grass roots level to move the trade unions to a more left-wing stance paid off when he was elected by a handsome majority over Gaitskell's candidate, George Brown.

In November 1956 Bevan got the post he really wanted: shadowing the Foreign Office. That year saw the Soviet invasion of Hungary and Anthony Eden's ill-judged invasion of the Suez Canal, which cost the Prime Minister his job. Both crises revealed Bevan at his thoughtful and eloquent best, which helped persuade a reluctant Gaitskell to bow to the growing pressure to offer him the Foreign Office portfolio.

If Bevan could not have the leadership, shadow Foreign Secretary was the job he most wanted; but it brought him the greatest unhappiness of his entire turbulent political career. At the National Executive Committee he had championed unilateral nuclear disarmament – and lost. He must either speak at Labour's annual conference, this time in Brighton, for the executive's position or resign as shadow Foreign Secretary. Resignation meant not simply throwing aside all his own hopes for the things he could achieve as Foreign Secretary in the Labour government, which he believed was going to be elected soon, but also splitting the Party again after he had managed to overcome Gaitskell's mistrust and unite it.

Jennie and Michael Foot were adamant he should resign rather than abandon unilateralism. They had always been more convinced of the unilateralist case than Bevan. But all three knew the destructive venom his old friends would turn on him for his apostasy if Bevan supported the Party line. 'I am just about to save this Party,' he told Jennie, 'but I shall destroy myself in doing so.'[76] Close as they were to him, Jennie and Foot failed to understand the mindset of a man who had sat in the Labour Cabinet and watched the nuclear programme begin; who had never entirely shared their straightforward determination that Britain should be a non-nuclear state. For Bevan, the issue was not quite so black and white.

With his oldest and closest friends sitting in the hall and hanging on every word, he told the conference: 'If you carry this resolution and follow out all its implications and do not run away from it, you will send a Foreign Secretary, whoever he may be, naked into the conference chamber.' It was not statesmanship, he said, 'but an emotional spasm.' To his old friends, it was betrayal. Those close to him, like Michael Foot, though perhaps he did not quite mean it: 'How much the deed was premeditated, no one will ever know; the theme, yes, of course; but the actual words, the lash laid about our backs; who could tell whether that was premeditated?' Later in the speech, says Foot, 'he paused and surveyed the most tremulous, heartbroken audience he had ever addressed in his life, and he would not relent.'[77] Much of the rest of Bevan's speech was drowned out by furious shouts from the floor. 'Bevan into Bevin,' said the *Daily Telegraph* and it was right: it could might have been Ernest Bevin, telling the Cabinet that it must develop an atom bomb because 'I don't want any other Foreign Secretary of this country to be talked at by a Secretary of State in the US as I have just had in my discussions with Mr Byrnes.'

The break that probably caused him the most pain was with his old friend Michael Foot, the editor of *Tribune*, who used the paper to denounce his old mentor. 'I was furious with Michael,' writes Jennie. 'Michael had richly earned the right to have his point of view forcefully stated. But what about Nye? Had he no rights? Were only letters and comments traducing his point of view to be published?'[78]

Bevan and Gaitskell coexisted. The shadow Cabinet had an anti-Bevanite majority, but Bevan was able to move them, almost imperceptibly, to slightly more radical positions than they might otherwise have adopted, especially on foreign affairs.

He was in Moscow with Gaitskell in 1959 when Prime Minister Harold Macmillan announced a general election to be held on 8 October 1959. The sixty-two-year-old Bevan threw himself into campaigning, concentrating his own speeches mostly on foreign affairs. According to Michael Foot, Bevan could not trust himself to speak on domestic affairs, believing that a Gaitskell government would make no reforms he considered worthwhile. 'One is bound to be frightened of what one might say. A large meeting has its dangers. You are sometimes tempted to say things you shouldn't say,' he privately admitted to the journalist Geoffrey Goodman. 'Public life now is becoming an intolerable burden with few redeeming features. If it goes on we shall all degenerate into pure salesmen – like the American politicians.'[79] He was also hampered by an undiagnosed illness, which made him lethargic and seemed to cause him pain.

Labour lost, as expected. Gaitskell came to lunch at the

Bevans' farmhouse in the country and asked if he would stand for deputy leader. Bevan agreed. The following day Michael Foot and his wife came for lunch, Foot nursing his wounds from his failure to be elected at Plymouth Devonport. 'No prodigal son was ever welcomed with such a feast as my wife and I had at Asheridge that gloomy weekend,' he wrote.[80]

Meanwhile Gaitskell had drawn his own conclusions from Labour's defeat, as summarized in an article by his ally Douglas Jay. Socialism was dead and in order to make itself electable the Labour Party should never again mention further nationalization and should consider changing its name from Labour to Radical. As preparation for making fundamental changes to his party, Gaitskell announced a proposal at Labour's conference in Blackpool later that year to remove Clause Four of the Party's constitution, which promised 'the common ownership of the means of production, distribution and exchange.'

He never managed to get it through and the clause remained until Tony Blair became leader in 1992 and campaigned against it. Blair was attacked by elderly Bevanites such as Barbara Castle and Michael Foot, but Bevan himself had chosen a different course in his conference speech. He was still shadow Foreign Secretary and Gaitskell's new deputy. He had come too far to abandon Gaitskell now unless he had to. He maintained (and it was far from easy) that Gaitskell's speech contained a 'very important ingredient of unity.' Gaitskell was right: many of the electorate had said they did not vote Labour because of nationalization. But was that their real reason? And even if it was, should the Party abandon its long-held beliefs the moment they stopped being fashionable?

Bevan got through the speech without saying anything disloyal, but there was no doubt that Gaitskell had opened up a new battleground between them. How would Bevan choose to fight it?

We will never know. Soon after the conference he went into the Royal Free Hospital in Gray's Inn Road, London, for a four-hour operation for malignant cancer. Michael Foot visited him immediately afterwards. 'He had all the tubes and paraphernalia stuck in his sides and could not speak or give any real sign of recognition. He was like a great tree hacked down, wantonly, in full leaf.'[81]

Bevan and Jennie believed that the strains and tensions of the past few years had brought on his illness. 'He was too proud to show his wounds in public,' she wrote, 'and in private what he cared about was hiding from me as much as he could of the abuse that was being heaped on him.'[82]

The operation was unsuccessful, but Jennie decided Nye should not know he was dying. In March 1960 he was well enough to talk to some journalists, one of whom asked if he was writing his memoirs. 'I strongly disapprove of people in active public life writing their memoirs,' he answered. And to his old Tredegar friend Archie Rush, who knew the truth, he said: 'I want to live because there are one or two things I want to do.'[83] Jennie bought some summer dresses to encourage the illusion that they would soon be setting off for the South of France where he could recuperate in time to face whatever the Labour Party and Hugh Gaitskell had in store at the Scarborough conference.

On 7 July 1960 Aneurin Bevan passed away. 'Nye is asleep next door,' Jennie wrote to Michael Foot. 'Later today he will be taken home to Wales. Tomorrow he will be cremated in keeping with his known views.' There would be no church ceremony, for Bevan:

... was never a hypocrite. No falsity must touch him once he is no longer able to defend his views. He was not a cold-blooded rationalist. He was no calculating machine. He was a great humanist whose religion lay in loving his fellow men and trying to serve them. He could kneel reverently in chapel, synagogue, Eastern mosque, Catholic cathedral on occasions when friends called him there for marriage or dedication or burial services. He knelt reverently in respect to a friend or friend's faith, but he never pretended to be anything other than what he was, a humanist.[84]

Bevan's Legacy and the Twenty-first Century

Today it is difficult to imagine a Britain in which it is impossible to have hospital treatment. Day-to-day experience for poor people includes hip replacements and doctor's visits. Children rarely have polio and almost never have tuberculosis. The illnesses caused by squalor, malnutrition and dirt are no longer common. It is assumed that most people, especially the elderly, will have a roof over their head and adequate health care. Political squabbles revolve around who should pay for it, not whether it should be available.

This level of comfort, which we take for granted, is a direct result of the work of the 1945 Labour government. The infrastructure and the principle that created the Welfare State also created a step change from the pre-war notion of personal responsibility, by which the Government only stepped into small arenas at certain times, subsidizing houses for council tenants or sponsoring a hospital. The unified principle behind the Welfare State has created a nation in which people expect a unified response to need.

But this does not mean that we have socialism. Bevan's socialism is a rare and delicate thing. It is, he wrote, 'essentially cool in temper. It sees the individual in his context with society and is therefore compassionate and tolerant. Because it knows that all political action must be a choice between a number of possible alternatives it eschews all absolute proscriptions and final decisions.'[85] It depends absolutely on democracy: not only through the formal enfranchisement of working-class groups, but day-to-day enfranchisement in all the decisions that affect the conditions in which working people live. Perhaps more importantly, it has at its heart the advancement of individuals and so the advancement of society as a whole.

Coupled with this, for Bevan, was an absolute belief in human nature. Given conditions of security and enfranchisement, people would respond by supporting each other and contributing to society. Only where some people held power and others did not were social relationships warped by self-interest. 'Where wealth is concentrated in a few hands the outcome is ostentatious spending and the meretricious glamour that goes with it.' The glamour and excitement created by conspicuous consumption was a fallacy.

> The attempt of democratic socialism to universalize
> the consumption of the best that society can afford
> meets with resistance from those whose sense of values
> is deformed by the daily parade of functionless wealth.
> When wealth is dispersed and distributed in scores
> of millions of homes the result is not so conspicuous.
> The social scene provides fewer dramatic contrasts. But
> there is no doubt about which type of society produces
> more quiet contentment and political stability.[86]

This belief is the first clue to the reasons why Bevan's grand palace is perhaps now a grand façade. When

Margaret Thatcher was elected in 1979 her view of what made a settled and peaceful country could not have been more different. The Market Liberal principle to encourage entrepreneurs and create opportunity struck at the heart of Bevan's socialism. 'Far more desirable,' said Thatcher at a 1978 Conservative conference, 'and more practical than the pursuit of equality is the pursuit of equality of opportunity. Opportunity means nothing unless it includes the right to be unequal ... Let our children grow tall – and some grow taller than others, if they have it in them to do so.'[87]

This shift to the Right decimated Bevan's housing policy, which depended on public ownership and accountability, on using local authorities as his organizing tool and on central funding as a unifying force. The Thatcher government made the sale of council housing a priority. Bevan's houses were the most desirable and therefore the most vulnerable to private ownership.

Post-war social change has eaten away at the dream of new towns as well. Bevan made access to housing dependent on the family unit and on local employment. Local authorities interpreted this to mean deserving working-class families with wage-earning husbands. The result was institutionalized inequality, with single parents, unemployed people and new immigrant families denied access to the best council housing.

The Housing Act of 1952, under a Conservative government, increased local authorities' subsidy, but recreated links between local authority housing and the working class by limiting council housing to slum clearance and rehousing. In 1956 the Housing Subsidies Act introduced incentives for

137

local councils to build high-rise developments – in direct opposition to the Bevan dream of affordable, good-quality, spacious housing. So, by stages, Bevan's peaceful, hard-working towns and socialist villages were eaten away.

The best housing became owner-occupied. People moved from areas where they could not buy and were replaced by groups with less of a stake in the community. Council housing became linked with poverty and poor-quality 'system building'.

The Housing Homeless Persons Act (1985) placed more strain on council housing. It made local authorities prioritize the homeless in their lettings policy – again linking council housing and deprivation and filling Bevan's homes with poor and socially stigmatized groups. In the meantime, successive governments reduced expenditure on the maintenance and replacement of homes.

The final blow to Bevan's dream of public ownership and affordable, accessible housing came with the growth and reliance on housing associations. In 1964 the Housing Corporation was formed with the ability to convert government funding into loans for housing associations. In 1974 a Labour government increased the Corporation's powers to include regulating housing association properties and tenancies. Since 1979 the direct role of local authorities has been reduced, until in 1987 the introduction of Housing Action Trusts completed the task of shifting the focus for providing homes from the local authorities to the housing associations, funded and controlled by a non- governmental central authority.

And so Bevan's refusal to consider a national housing

body was subverted and undermined. It is these shifts in policy that have caused us to enter a new century with the old problems of homelessness, inequality, regeneration, and a lack of affordable housing still on the social agenda.

Perhaps Bevan's reforms were also undermined by a change in working class values. Some have argued that it was the socialist preference for public over private that sowed the seeds of failure for the housing dream. The British public rejected tenancies – no matter how afford-able or how good the quality – in favour of home owner-ship. This was also the reasoning behind the sale of council housing in the 1980s.

But what were tenants rejecting? Bevan's dream was for mixed estates where all people could share in the commu-nity. The houses were excellent, so it was not the housing that tenants rejected in favour of struggling to meet mort-gage re-payments. Perhaps it was the planners, who built without thought for schools and shops or even for the mothers who might not always be available to supervise children in communal play. Perhaps it was the administra-tors of the local authorities themselves, who let housing first to the well-off worker rather than the needy. Bevan's understanding of human nature was rooted in pre-war working class solidarity and a little Welsh village. His dream reflected this, but the mood of the times did not.

Housing statistics bear out this story. In 1938 – before the Second World War and before Bevan – 32 per cent of housing was owner-occupied and 11 per cent was local authority tenancies. By 1979, however, 56 per cent was owner-occupied, but 29 per cent was let by local authorities.

In 2002, 70 per cent were owner-occupied and council tenancies offered only 13 per cent. (However, private renting has reduced steadily over these years – from 57 per cent in 1938 to 10 per cent in 2002.)[88] This picture is not improved by the 40,000 local authority houses that are unfit for habitation. Between 1979 and 2002, 2,487,000 local authority homes have passed into private ownership.

Perhaps the most constant of Bevan's principles was a planned approach to housing. The idea of planning new building so that the environment could be protected is so much part of current thought that it is hard to imagine cities without open spaces and green belts. A 2003 Labour government policy states: 'Our objective is to ensure that everyone has the opportunity of a decent home and so promote social cohesion, well-being and self-dependence.'[89] Room and space requirements are again part of policy and practice. New towns are once more on the policy agenda. The central provider is the registered social landlord who is accountable to the Government. A proportion of government spending is given to the housing corporation, which allocates it to registered social landlords. So the principle of accountability for spending on housing has been retained, but at one step removed from direct government responsibility.

It is hard to say how Bevan would have reacted to this. Certainly, his view that spending and direct accountability must be linked has been undermined, but on the other hand the Government still has responsibility to provide housing for everyone. Home ownership is the 'gold standard' of policy makers, but money is spent on rented provision and that provision is public and monitored, as the drop in private renting shows. Town planning and new towns are here, but they do not stress the mixed social housing and 'English village' that Bevan envisaged.

Perhaps the biggest difficulty for Bevan would be the absolute link between social housing and social need. Despite New Labour's attempts to ensure that builders of new private estates include social housing, people in need are often housed together and separated from the rest of society. One of the present authors actually lives in an estate divided in this way: a small cluster of housing association homes for the elderly and disabled built by a private builder, and divided from the private estate by fences and planning.

Bevan believed that democratic socialism would fill the gap left by the destruction of capitalist economies during the war, if only governments kept their nerve and their confidence. He also wanted passionately to raise the standard of individual life and this he achieved. Perhaps he would view current policy as an acceptable accommodation to the post-war political reality, but he would be passionately opposed to the inequality of twenty- first-century housing.

Council housing fell victim to a new political ideology. Damage to the NHS was the direct result of a Labour government: Bevan's resignation was over prescription and dental charges. Nevertheless, the NHS still provided treatment free at the point of delivery and was the biggest single employer in the country and possibly the world.

In the 1970s it fell to Barbara Castle to undertake the next round in creating an NHS that did not discriminate between patients because of their income. Bevan was dead, but the 'pay-bed' issue resurfaced. In 1945 Bevan had bought off the consultants to ensure they would spend time in public hospitals. In 1974 the one-time Bevanite Castle and Harold Wilson's government pledged to remove private practice from the NHS. They were thwarted by the consultants, who saw the phasing out of paid beds as a threat to private practice and their professional status.

For the first time ever the consultants took industrial action in the form of a work-to-rule, in defence of private medicine. Simultaneously, public service unions took guerrilla action against private beds in public hospitals. This division was not part of the negotiations in 1945 and is a measure of how far Britain and its people had moved from the optimistic and determined post-war electorate. The result was agreement from the Government to a slow reduction of private beds in public hospitals.

This allowed private medicine time to regroup. The percentage of beds reserved for private medicine had fallen to less than 1 per cent, but between 1974 and 1979 it rose steadily, despite Prime Minister Wilson's attempts to phase out private medicine.

In exactly the scenario that Bevan had sought to avoid, consultants walked out of public hospitals and into private ones. When the Thatcher government encouraged private insurance schemes in 1980, the groundwork of a separate service had already been laid. In 2002 the consultants once again refused new contracts that would establish preferable rates of pay dependant on changes in conditions of service.

Bevan's nationalization of the NHS had another

unintended effect, which has undermined his intentions over the years: it created the largest employer and bureaucracy the world had ever seen. The NHS was run centrally and was responsible for services as different as large inner-city hospitals, nurses working across broad geographic areas and individual dental and optical businesses. It consumed a vast amount of equipment and required huge investment in infrastructure.

Bevan believed that such a structure could be managed and controlled by civil servants – in fact, it had to be in order to retain public accountability. He also believed that the structure would be self-limiting: as the British people grew healthier and stronger, demand on the NHS would lessen.

> The question uppermost in my mind at that time was whether a consistent pattern of behaviour would reveal itself among the millions using the service and how long it would take for this to emerge? Unless this happened fairly soon, it would not be possible to put in reliable estimates for the budget. [But] ordinary men and women were aware of what was happening. They knew from their own experience that a considerable portion of the initial expenditure ... was the result of past neglect.[90]

But despite increasing management control during the 1980s, the NHS has not been able to make economies and to limit spending reliably. And a growing population, with growing expectations of medicine, has continued to increase demand. Bevan might reply that this is because the encouragement of wealth among the few has distorted the desires of the many, and perhaps it has.

Health centres – which Bevan planned, but which were only opened after the 1950s – have been much more successful. Following Bevan's principle that health care should be preventative as well as curative, health centres provide access to a doctor, but also baby clinics, dietary information, nurses and much more. Their size and which services they should offer is still debated. Most recently, some centres have opened cafés and coffee bars offering healthy food for pensioners or children. Today health centres are at the forefront of the debate about the role of nurses in primary health care. Should the nurses in health centres take over routine health care, administer injections and first aid, even make out routine prescriptions?

Health care through health centres and doctors, backed up by a system of nurses and receptionists and also offering clinics, is an enduring legacy of Bevan's NHS. In Bevan's view, health care reaching out to ordinary people was essential to democratic socialism. Although the NHS has seen many changes over the last fifty years, the idea of health centres has flourished.

They are as yet untouched by New Labour proposals that strike at the very heart of Bevan's intentions, like foundation hospitals. Bevan was determined that the best hospital care should be available to everybody: 'The essence of a satisfactory health service is that the rich and the poor are treated alike, that poverty is not a disability, and wealth is not an advantage.'[91] Current New Labour policy introduces foundation status to the best-performing hospitals: they will have more money and less central interference. It is easy to foresee that these foundation hospitals will become the best and most desirable centres of care – open to some and not to others.

The former Labour Health Secretary Frank Dobson (1940–2019) has defended the Bevanite view, saying that the policy of foundation hospitals 'gets things back to front: the priority should be to bring less-successful hospitals up to the standards of the best. This proposal will help the best get better, while the less successful fall further behind. It will widen the performance gap and generate inequalities.' And foundation hospitals 'will promote local and regional inequalities, widen the performance gap and introduce a two-tier hospital service. The NHS deserves better than an idea based on the new pronouncements "To them that hath shall be given" and "Please don't mind the gap".'[92] We can almost hear Bevan rumbling in the background: 'The essence of a satisfactory health service is that the rich and the poor are treated alike.'[93]

The National Health Service – the greatest experiment in socialism of the 1945 government – is still free at the point of delivery for services except prescriptions, opticians and dental treatment. Doctors still visit patients at home without charge, although their new contract limits those patients' access to 'out-of-hours' services. Our grandmother would still not need the coins in her button tin. Hospitals still treat everyone who comes to their door. Great diseases are eradicated by a comprehensive programme of education and vaccination. The working population is healthier than at any other time in history. Most people have access to a health centre.

But not all hospitals give the same service. Patients who can pay have access to care that other patients cannot have. Where you live affects your health services. We are well on the way to the 'two-tier' system that Bevan so firmly rejected.

Running the unwieldy leviathan of the NHS has always been a political problem. Perhaps the last straw was the scandal of unsatisfactory care unearthed during the Wilson government. While the NHS as a whole might be democratically answerable, individual service providers for the old or the mentally ill were not. Tales of lost or misused equipment and low standards of patient care were legendary. The very structure of the NHS – split between doctors who retained professional autonomy, other health care workers like nurses in salaried employment and managers and ancillary staff employed by the state – rendered it unaccountable. Margaret Thatcher's solution – to create small pools of management separate from doctors – was unsatisfactory, even from her Market Liberal perspective. Her legacy was a divided and inefficient NHS harried by increases in private insurance. Today the NHS still struggles to function efficiently, but it is still here, albeit rather battered and bruised.

Bevan's council houses and his NHS were massive and lasting achievements such as very few politicians can boast. His imprint on the fabric of our society is greater than that of any but two or three twentieth century politicians. Few of them can claim that their work changed fundamentally the way their countrymen live. Apart from Bevan, the claim can be made for Attlee and Thatcher and perhaps by those who laid the foundations for the achievements of Attlee's government, David Lloyd George (1863–1945) and the now almost forgotten Sir Henry Campbell-Bannerman (1836–1908). They all became Prime Minister. Bevan may be the only non-Prime Minister with a similar claim.

He was a great minister. Both his achievements and his civil servants testify to that. But the legacy of Bevan as a politician is less certain and more debatable. The leaders of the Left of the Labour Party have often been inspirational figures, like James Maxton in the 1920s or Tony Benn in the 1980s. Bevan, too, was inspirational, but he was a very different character. He was not a natural rebel. He avoided Maxton's embrace in the 1929 parliament and it's a fair bet that he would have avoided Benn's embrace in that of 1979, as did Bevan's disciple Michael Foot. Whereas Maxton allowed his followers to become a kind of exclusive sect that eventually split from the Labour Party and the Bennites wrapped themselves in self-righteous sectarianism, Bevan never wanted to be in opposition. Richard Crossman was right: Bevan was a reluctant Bevanite. He frustrated many younger Bevanites such as Crossman and Foot by refusing to be their guru. His deepest conviction, the consideration which drove every political decision he made and which he reiterated throughout his life, remains what he told Jennie in 1931: 'I tell you, it's the Labour Party or nothing.'

Yet Bevan got himself expelled from the Labour Party during the war and only escaped a second expulsion in the 1950s because of Attlee's quiet determination to keep him.

And, whether he liked it or not, Bevan was at the centre of the Bevanite sect. He allowed himself to be manoeuvred into rebellions over comparatively minor matters. He resigned from the Government on the issue of charging for teeth and spectacles, which hardly undermined the principle of a free NHS.

In short, he fell into a trap set for him by Gaitskell, Morrison and their trade union sponsors such as Arthur Deakin. 'In a sense,' writes Gaitskell's biographer Brian Brivati, 'Nye Bevan was the making of Hugh Gaitskell.'[94] Without the giant Bevan to slay, Gaitskell might well not have become Labour leader. If Bevan had not consented to be slain, he might have become Labour leader, as Attlee privately wanted. Later, Bevan rebelled over unilateralism, a cause in which he only half believed. He failed to choose between being Labour's conscience and being a pragmatic politician who sometimes has to make shoddy compromises to get things done.

In 1945 Attlee gave Bevan a real job to do and he did it brilliantly. No other Labour Prime Minister in history would have brought Bevan in from the cold so decisively. Ramsay MacDonald, James Callaghan (1912–2005), Tony Blair, even Harold Wilson would not have taken into the highest levels of government the 'enfant terrible' of the Left; a man who had only recently been readmitted to the Party after being expelled for rebellion. That Attlee took the risk in 1945 reflects well on him. That it paid off in work that benefited thousands of British people is an equally great tribute to Nye Bevan.

As a rebel leader, perhaps because his heart was never in

it, Bevan failed to move Labour to a more radical stance; and he also failed to limit the damage the split did to the Party. Of course it takes two to argue and there's plenty of evidence that the venom of the Right was at least as much to blame as that of the Left, if not more so. Hugh Gaitskell does not come out of any sober analysis of the Bevanite split with much credit: he was a schemer who admitted he could not count on the support of the unions without doing some of their dirty work for them.

Near the end of his life Bevan seems to have come to some sort of accommodation with Gaitskell. Just before his death, he appears to have been preparing himself to head off a damaging split as Gaitskell launched an ill-judged and ill-timed attack on Clause Four of the Party's constitution.

The Bevanite rebellion had one lasting legacy, though it is far from certain whether Bevan would have approved. He wanted to show trade union members how leaders like Arthur Deakin were using the block vote to stifle radicalism in the Party, thereby ensuring the defeat of left-wing candidates like himself. Before he died, Bevan had at least seen the all-powerful union barons consulting with the members of their delegations before they cast their votes at a Labour Party conference. In 1956, he was narrowly elected Labour Party treasurer at the Party conference thanks to the fact that some trade unions defied their leaders and cast their votes in the way their members wanted.

'Never again,' wrote Michael Foot apocalyptically, 'would a few trade union leaders meeting in private behind the backs of the rest of the Party be able to distribute offices and determine policy according to their whim. Henceforth trade union leaders would increasingly appear not as a praetorian guard shielding the leader, but as independent forces whose allegiance and enthusiasm and votes must be enlisted precisely because they themselves had become responsive to their own rank and file: a development most healthy for democracy.'[95]

Well, perhaps. Foot, of course, wrote that long before he was elected Labour Party leader in 1982. He then had to watch everything he had worked hard to build be destroyed by the horrific spectacle of big trade unions conducting ballots on whether Tony Benn or Dennis Healey (1917–2015) should become the Party's deputy leader. It helped to ensure the downfall both of the unions and of the socialist soul of the Labour Party that Bevan had fought for.

One might accuse Bevan of mishandling the Labour Party in the last decade of his life, but it cannot be denied he is one of the few political giants Britain has produced and one of the most humane and attractive of politicians. He inspired the sort of loyalty that only very special politicians can command. Michael Foot, himself a considerable politician and an intelligent man with an exceptionally well-stocked mind, wrote a biography of Bevan which is like no other: huge, sprawling, literate, informative and every line reeking of hero-worship. Roy Hattersley remarks a little acidly that he could not understand why 'a first-rate Michael Foot would spend his life trying to be a second-rate Nye Bevan', but he did not know Bevan the way Foot did.[96] And Foot, though he mistakenly thought Bevan could do no wrong, deserves to have the last word on him:

> For socialism, for those of us who heard him speak and talk and argue and who shared his political aspirations, he was the man who did more than any other of his age to keep alive the idea of democratic socialism. With him, it never lost its power as a revolutionary creed. Others might define it as well or serve it as faithfully. But no one else, for most of us, could give it a vibrant and audacious quality and make it the most ambitious and intelligent and civilized of modern doctrines.[97]

Endnotes

1   Keir Starmer, on Labour's vision for NHS, Speech in Braintree, Essex, 22 May 2023
2   Ibid.
3   Aneurin Bevan in *Plebs Magazine* (1921).
4   Aneurin Bevan, *In Place of Fear*, (London, 1952).
5   John Campbell, *Nye Bevan: A Biography*, (London, 1997).
6   Bevan, *In Place of Fear*.
7   Campbell, *Nye Bevan: A Biography*.
8   Michael Foot, *Aneurin Bevan* (n.p., 1997).
9   Foot, *Aneurin Bevan*.
10 Ibid.
11 Campbell, *Nye Bevan: A Biography*, p.39.
12 Ibid.
13 Beatrice Webb, *Diaries,* (n.p., 2001).
14 Foot, *Aneurin Bevan*.
15 Patricia Hollis, *Jennie Lee: A Life*, (Oxford, 1997).
16 Foot, *Aneurin Bevan*.
17 Jennie Lee, *My Life with Nye,* (London, 1981).
18 *Tribune*, July 1937.
19 Lee, *My Life with Nye*.
20 Francis Beckett, *Clem Attlee* (London, 2015).
21 Clement Attlee, *As It Happened* (Surrey, 1954).
22 *Tribune*, 1 August 1941.
23 Foot, *Aneurin Bevan*.

24 Hollis, *Jennie Lee: A Life.*

25 *Tribune*, 2 October 1942.

26 Beckett, *Clem Attlee.*

27 Beckett, *Clem Attlee.*

28 Leah Manning, *A Life for Education*, (London, 1970), p.164.

29 Peter Hennessy, *Never Again: Britain 1945–1951* (London, 1992), p.56.

30 Picture Post, 4 January 1941.

31 Aneurin Bevan, *Why Not Trust The Tories?*, (London, 1944).

32 Lee, *My Life with Nye.*

33 Barbara Castle, *Fighting All The Way*, (London, 1993), p.125–7.

34 Foot, *Aneurin Bevan.*

35 Bevan, *In Place of Fear.*

36 Foot, *Aneurin Bevan.*

37 Ibid.

38 Ibid.

39 Ibid.

40 Hennessy, *Never Again: Britain 1945–51.*

41 Bevan, *Why Not Trust the Tories?*

42 Hennessy, *Never Again: Britain 1945–51.*

43 Kenneth Harris, *Attlee*, (London, 1982).

44 Lee, *My Life with Nye.*

45 Bevan, *Why Not Trust the Tories?*

46 Foot, *Aneurin Bevan.*

47 Campbell, *Nye Bevan: A Biography.*

48 Hennessy, *Never Again: Britain 1945–51.*

49 Foot, *Aneurin Bevan.*

50 Ibid.

51 Bevan, *In Place of Fear*.

52 Foot, *Aneurin Bevan*.

53 Jones and Lowe, *From Beveridge to Blair: the first 50 years of Britain's welfare state 1948–1998* (Manchester, 2002).

54 *The Times* (5 July 1948).

55 Bevan, *In Place of Fear*, p.122.

56 Ibid.

57 Ibid.

58 Foot, *Aneurin Bevan*.

59 Bevan, *Why Not Trust the Tories?*

60 Foot, *Aneurin Bevan*.

61 Bevan, *In Place of Fear*.

62 Ibid.

63 Hennessy, *Never Again*.

64 Bevan, *In Place of Fear*.

65 Ibid.

66 Ibid.

67 Foot, *Aneurin Bevan*.

68 Ibid.

69 Henry Pelling, *A Short History of the Labour Party* (London, 1965).

70 Harris, *Attlee*.

71 Hollis, *Jennie Lee*.

72 Brian Brivati, *Hugh Gaitskell* (London, 1996).

73 Janet Morgan, ed, *The Backbench Diaries of Richard Crossman* (London, 1981).

74 Dalton's diary, 3 February 1952.

75 Foot, *Aneurin Bevan*.

76 Lee, *My Life with Nye*.

77 Foot, *Aneurin Bevan*.

78 Lee, *My Life with Nye*.

79 Foot, *Aneurin Bevan*.

80 Ibid.

81 Foot, *Aneurin Bevan*.

82 Lee, *My Life with Nye*.

83 Foot, *Aneurin Bevan*.

84 Lee, *My Life with Nye*.

85 Bevan, *In Place of Fear*.

86 Ibid.

87 Margaret Thatcher, Conservative Party Conference 1978.

88 Figures from the office of the Deputy Prime Minister.

89 Office of the Deputy Prime Minister: http://www. housing.odpm. gov.uk/information/index.htm.

90 Bevan, *In Place of Fear*.

91 Ibid.

92 Frank Dobson in *The Guardian*, 4 June 2002.

93 Bevan, *In Place of Fear*.

94 Brian Brivati, *Hugh Gaitskell*, (London, 1996).

95 Foot, *Aneurin Bevan*.

96 Roy Hattersley, Who Goes Home? (London, 1996).

97 Michael Foot, Aneurin Bevan.

Index

introduction of Welfare State, 137; Bevan's view of, 100–101, 106, 112; 1950 election, 112; 1951 election, 115, 117; 1951 government, 120–122; 1955 election, 127

Cook, Arthur James, 15

Council of Europe, 107

Cripps, Sir Stafford, 36, 39, 44;
and Unity Campaign, 44, 46; launches Tribune, 46; united front campaign, 49–50; expelled from Labour Party, 50; supports war, 49, 50; political advancement, 59; readmitted to Labour Party, 70; in post-war Labour government, 76–77, 81, 112–114; death, 114

Crossman, Richard, 119, 121, 147; and nuclear weapons, 125–126; defects to Gaitskell, 128

Czechoslovakia, 48

D

Daily Express, 22, 25

Daily Herald, 19, 22, 49

Daily Mirror, 55, 128

Daily Telegraph, 131

Daily Worker, 53

Dalton, Hugh, 71, 75–76. 81, 113;
ousted from NEC, 118; on Bevan's parliamentary performances, 122

Deakin, Arthur, 118–120, 123, 124–128;
demands Bevan's expulsion, 148–149

defence spending, 111, 114, 123

Depression, 67–69, 81

Dobson, Frank, 2, 145

Driberg, Tom, 118–119, 121, 125;

Dublin, 22

E

Ebbw Vale, 14, 16, 24, 58

Economist, 121

Eden, Anthony, 64–65, 123, 127, 129

Egypt, 123

El Alamein, 57

Empire Windrush, 3, 107

Epping, 68

European Union, 107

Evening Standard, 23, 25

Health, 1–2, 10, 16, 22–23,
   61, 69, 72–73, 82, 84–85,
   90–99, 102–103, 107–108,
   110, 113–114, 116, 122, 135,
   143–146, 150;
   centres, 76, 95, 97, 144;
   consultants, 90–91,
   96–98, 142; curative
   medicine, 73, 82, 84;
   general practitioners,
   5, 91–97; hospitals, 1,
   5, 76, 82, 83, 90–92,
   96–98, 142–146;
   prescription charges,
   112–113, 115–116;
   preventative medicine,
   2, 73, 82, 84; private
   medicine, 142; see also
   National Health Service
Henderson, Arthur, 21, 31;
   becomes Labour leader,
   32; loses seat, 33
Hennessy, Peter, 79
Hitler, Adolf, 1, 38, 43, 45,
   93;
   becomes Chancellor, 38;
   annexation of Austria,
   48; Munich Agreement,
   48; invades Soviet
   Union, 53; defeat, 57
Ho Chi Minh, 123
Holland, 68

homelessness, 139
Horner, Arthur, 9
housing, 14, 22–23, 72–73,
   76, 82, 84–89, 92, 98–99,
   105, 108–111, 113, 122,
   137–141;
   associations, 138; under
   Conservatives, 85, 87,
   122, 137–139; council,
   86, 88, 98, 109, 137–139,
   141; and immigrants, 3,
   107, 137; pre-fabricated,
   86; private, 141; social,
   84, 141; statistics, 139;
   war damage, 67, 69, 74,
   85, 97, 109
Hungary, 129

I
immigrants, 3, 107
Independent Labour Party
   (ILP), 20, 24, 27, 33–34,
   36;
   split with Labour Party,
   20, 23–24, 26–27, 145;
   in Unity Campaign,
   43; opposes war, 50;
   members in post-war
   Labour government,
   70; ideological purity,
   37, 121
India, 59, 123